CHRIST

꙳ AT THE ꙳

DOOR

Published by Crest Books

Crest Books
The Salvation Army National Headquarters
615 Slaters Lane
Alexandria, VA 22313
Phone: 703/684-5523

Lt. Col. Allen Satterlee, Editor-in-Chief and National Literary Secretary
Roger O. Selvage Jr., Art Director
Jessica Curtis, Editorial Assistant

Available in print from crestbooks.com.

ISBN: 978-1-946709-04-251495

Cover Image: *Light of the World*, c.1851-53, oil on canvas, by William Holman Hunt
(1827-1910); Keble College, Oxford, UK

Printed in the United States

CHRIST AT THE DOOR

Biblical Keys to Our Salvationist Future

A Resource for Helping Salvationists Revitalize Themselves & Their Corps

by PHIL NEEDHAM

FOREWORD

Phil and Keitha Needham are among our best friends. Their life together is a testimony to the grace, peace, and hope of God. They live well the life that Phil shares in all of his remarkable writings.

Christ at the Door is his best. It shares well his compassion and wisdom, his thoughtfulness and kindness, and his insights and suggestions. It shares most helpful ways forward for the time and place in which we live.

We enjoyed the churched culture of an earlier time. The prestige, the prerogatives, the pedestal, and the power were relished. We now live in a mission culture. The Christian movement was born in such a culture. This is where we (and especially The Salvation Army!) began, and this is where we are most at home.

In *Christ at the Door* Phil shares a most helpful and useful under-standing of who we are and whose we are. It is filled with insights, gifts, and blessings for this time. Phil views the whole of the world God gives us. He gives us confidence and assured hope for the present and the future. I am confident *Christ at the Door* will stir and lead many corps congregations to a new and stronger future. It will endure for years to come. It is a testament to Phil's wisdom, and equally, a testament to the life Phil and Keitha share with one another and with all who are blessed by their gifts.

May *Christ at the Door* bless your life, the lives of family and friends, and the Salvationist movement.

— **Kennon L. Callahan, Ph.D.**,
author, researcher, theologian, pastor

ACKNOWLEDGMENTS

This book is dedicated to a host of missional Salvationists who loved Jesus with such passion, believed him with such conviction, and poured out their lives for the world with such extravagance, they continue to this very day to be true models of what it means to be the-real-thing Salvationists. What they did at our beginnings, and what their spiritual descendants continue to do today, is to show us our calling—a calling to be both a community united in holy love and mutual support and also and quite naturally a community invading the world with the courage of sold-out disciples, the compassion of our Lord Jesus, and the hope of the gospel. They show us how to be a living movement more than a respected institution, a sold-out people more than a safe, protected church, radical followers of Jesus more than dutiful corps members. They remind us of our beginnings and they teach us the way to our future as a salvation army.

I also want to express my gratitude to the Clearwater, Florida Corps where we were invited to lead their annual Bible Conference last year. Following the conference I decided to expand the teaching material further, and this book is the result. I don't think the book would have come about without that invitation from Clearwater. Nor would it have happened without the tolerance, grace, and support of my wife Keitha, who gave me space and provided the first editing (She's the best in finding mistakes in the text that I manage to miss!). Most of all, I express gratitude to the Christ who beckons us all to follow Him and trusts us not only to bear His name but also to be Him in the world.

CONTENTS

WHY THIS BOOK?

Years ago I heard my friend and mentor Ken Callahan tell
the story of a congregation he was helping. He and the leaders of that church were praying together over the future of
a church that had had what Ken called "thirty-seven losing
seasons." As Ken put it, "We needed to gather all the prayer
we could." He describes what happened:

In the center wall of the chancel they have a remarkable
stained glass window of Christ standing at the door, knocking. You remember the picture by Holman. In the long, lost
church culture of an earlier time the understanding of the
window was, "Christ stands at the door, knocking, hoping
someone will hear the knock and come to the door, and open
the door and invite Christ **in** to their lives."

And, much was made of the fact that there was no door
knob or latchstring or keyhole on the outside of the door. We
would be the ones who would hear the knock and we would
come to the door and we would open the door and we would
invite Christ **in** to our lives.

It dawned on me that day as we were kneeling at the altar
rail, praying, with the sunlight streaming through the stained
glass window in a remarkable way, what the picture, the
window, the Biblical image means in our time: Christ stands
at the door, knocking, hoping someone will hear the knock,
and come to the door, and open the door so Christ can invite
them **out** into his life in mission.

Ken goes on to say that this particular congregation—and

many congregations, for that matter—emphasize only that we invite Christ into our hearts. They fail to see that we simply cannot have a private Christ. Crucial to the heart change we emphasize in The Salvation Army is the acquisition and cultivation of a heart for the world that God so loves (**John 3:16**). Ken closes with these words:

Good friends, it is no longer that we [only] invite Christ **in** to our lives. Now, Christ invites us **out into His life**. Where is Christ? In mission. Where does Christ live and die and is risen again and again? Among the human hurts and hopes God has planted all around us. Christ is in the world. When we are in the world, we are with Christ. It is not that we discover Christ; then, go and serve in mission. It is in the sharing of mission that we discover Christ. In this new day, Christ invites us **out**... to live and serve with him in mission. (*Twelve Keys to an Effective Church*. Second edition, pp. 53-54)

It strikes me that this image of Christ outside the door of the church, beckoning us to join Him in his mission for the world, is what the founders of our Salvation Army imagined. In fact, I believe it is an image that has never been more suitable for the whole church as it is today. As Ken says, "We live in the most promising mission field on the planet."

This invitation of Jesus is a calling to become His disciples, His church, and His mission. Properly understood, each of these callings is a calling *out*. Our calling to be His disciples is a summons to journey with him. Our calling to be His church is a calling to embody Him in the world. Our calling to be His mission is a calling to give ourselves to the world He loves. I propose that these are the keys to our Salvationist future.

The church has always lived in the age of mission. She has not, however, always recognized or embraced the mission. Our early Salvation Army did, and the result was our time of greatest growth and spiritual impact. Once we became settled (an institution), we started becoming more careful, cautious, and conservative, and therefore less consumed by our mission. This greater focus on internal matters was inevitable: We now had a large corporation to organize and maintain—and it was growing worldwide!

I thank God for this global Army of ours. It's a miracle of God. It's the fruit of dare-devil Salvationists who put their lives and reputations on the line, invaded foreign turf to share the love of Christ, and went after the poor, the destitute, and the exploited. They sang, "This shall be our battle song: There's salvation for the world!" (William James Pearson, *SASB*, 2015, Song 940) And they turned communities around the world upside down.

I believe this same missional passion of what we could call a gospel movement mentality can still be re-ignited. It's in our Salvationist DNA. There is a missional Salvationist latent in all of us, and Christ can release it. Our future depends on it. Christ is standing outside the doors of our corps, waiting for us to join him.

This book is designed to help Salvationists reclaim the heart of their calling as missional disciples of Jesus. It is a resource for Salvationists to use to envision a future both for themselves personally and for their corps. Its primary guiding resource is Scripture. The main concern is how we can best fulfill our calling to be a Biblically-based movement of holy, compassionate, disciple-making people. Along with this, the book explores ways in which our Salvation Army has exemplified that calling over the years, and what we can learn from that history. We look as well to some of the social changes that are currently shaping our world–and our corps!–in order to ask how they help us understand the best way forward as Salvationists faithful to our calling.

In order to help readers reflect on their own spiritual journey and calling, there are invitational questions at the end of each chapter providing for personal reflection and prayer over matters addressed in the chapter. There are also questions relating to the future of readers' corps. Readers may find that those questions open helpful discussions with other corps members as well as inform corps planning and action.

Hopefully these pages will both motivate individual Salvationists to explore areas for their own development as disciples of Jesus and also bring corps members together who are concerned about their corps and its future as a vital faith community and missional army. We hope it will sow seeds for radical corps renewal. The time is ripe for a reviving of the spiritual and missional revolution for which the early Army was so notorious and successful! The only meaningful location for this revolution is in the lives of individual Salvationists, in the faith community we call a corps, and in the world where faith and compassion are tested and proven. (I'm using "corps" to refer primarily to the specific faith communities for which we use that term in the Army, but also to any faith community within the spectrum of our diverse Army. For example, within the USA, it would refer also to that unique faith community called an Adult Rehabilitation Center.

Note: Scripture quotes in the book will be taken from the *Common English Bible* unless otherwise indicated. Readers, of course, are free to use the version they are familiar with and make comparisons.

WHERE WE ARE TODAY

The Salvation Army in the Western world is facing a crisis. Overall, membership has been declining for many years. Our concern in this book is not so much with the numbers: God excels in doing great things with a very small group–*if* the group is comprised of holy disciples who have been spiritually radicalized. To use Jesus' metaphor of the vineyard keeper who prunes the branches of the vines in order to stimulate greater future growth, we may want to claim that pruned as we are, an opportunity has now risen for new and more vital, healthy growth to sprout in our movement. In other words, exciting possibilities lie before us.

But alas, the membership decline in the Western world has been going on for so long it should concern us. Maybe God is trying to call us back to things we have forgotten.

There are forces that tend to desensitize us to our decline, or at least soften the blow. By and large, the public loves us, and I think that esteem has been well earned. We have a history of serving, helping, supporting, resourcing, and loving the marginalized. And we have frequently received generous support for it. I, for one, am proud of this well-earned esteem, and I'm glad that a historic commitment to the poor and mar-ginalized is so built into our organizational DNA, that we can't really shed it for the lure of upward mobility and still be "The Salvation Army."

The question we must ask ourselves is this: Is what the general public loves us for–our social work with the disad-vantaged–the reason we exist? If we go back to our earliest days, we find that this was not the bottom line for us. Yes, our missional target was primarily the marginalized. The urban poor made up the largest swath of the paganized population. And yes, early on very simple acts of material, economic, and social assistance occasionally took place, but not really as something separate from evangelism, rather as part of it. The bottom line was to bring the marginalized to Christian faith, and when the churches turned our converts away because they were, well, socially unpleasant to have around, our Army welcomed them back and we became a church for the marginalized.

We became both evangelizers and now disciplers, and it was better to combine these anyway. We became a church, not in the sense so many churches of that day were "church," closed societies and clubs with nice buildings. We became a missional church, a church existing for the sake of its mission in the world. And that mission was to make its converts sanctified, radical followers of Jesus Christ. *That* was the bottom line. (*Note:* Don't confuse our use of the word "radical" in this book with the sense in which it is most often used today to refer to a kind of political extremism. The word comes from a Latin word meaning "root, origin, source, or foundation." When we are being radical in this truest sense, we are being true to our origins, our roots.)

I have the sense that our Army in the West has too often strayed from this bottom line. And I think that is the primary reason we are declining. We are not making enough radical followers of Jesus Christ. You may be as profoundly concerned about this as I am. If not, perhaps as you read through these pages, both your concern and your hope will be awakened.

As we focus on Scripture that sheds light on our true calling, you may well be challenged to explore how we, as individual Salvationists and as corps communities, can better recapture that calling as a Salvation Army.

As this book is Bible-centered, let me make four comments about how we'll approach Scripture. First of all, I should point out that we will be jumping all around the Bible, not to cherry-pick but to give broader evidence for what I'm claiming Scripture is saying to us. Second, we'll read Scripture to understand it as accurately as we can with the Holy Spirit's help. That's important. Third, and even more importantly, we'll read Scripture to *be understood* by *it*. We'll read Scripture so that it can read *us* – read us personally, read us as a corps, and read us as a Salvation Army. We will ask Scripture to show us our true selves as followers of Jesus, and in the process, expose our false selves. **Please be sure you look up and carefully consider the Bible passages that are referenced throughout in bold. In other words, hear the Scripture for yourself rather than only through my interpretations! I recommend you do this as you read, perhaps pausing after a paragraph containing Bible references to read and reflect on the passages themselves. Or, if you'd rather keep the flow of your reading without stopping to read the Bible passages referenced, then you could go back after reading a chapter, or a section within a chapter, and then look up and reflect on the passages.**

The final comment about how we'll approach Scripture is that we shall take a cue from Samuel Logan Brengle. Our prophet of holiness said that when it comes to reading Scripture, we should not be concerned so much about increasing our mass of knowledge about the Bible. Rather, we should read it to kindle the flame of activating love in our hearts. Read the Bible, he said, not that you may know, but that you may *do* (*Helps to Holiness*, 24). The Bible calls us to obedience, and we shall call on Scripture not only to inspire us but also to challenge us, not only to bless us but also to activate us.

Remember when God changed Jacob's name? Jacob's name meant "Deceiver," and it was well earned. God said, I'm giving you a new name. You are now "Israel," meaning "the one who struggles with God," and I'm inflicting you with a big limp to remind you. So keep limping along, Israel, struggling with the Almighty for His blessing, and you'll find your calling.

The best thing that can happen through our engagement with this book and particularly with the God who calls and confronts us in Scripture, is that we learn our real name, the name that holds the key to how we walk this journey alongside Jesus, with all our limps and other evidences of inadequacy. A man named Cephas did just that, and learned that who he really was is Peter, God's "Rock," a rock that held even though he wavered more than once. A man named Saul did, now as Paul, and he brought the Gospel to the Mediterranean world, with a limp he called his "thorn in the flesh."

We all have our limps and limitations. And God says, bring them with you to the front lines, and I will make you and your corps into a salvation people.

PART ONE:

THE JOURNEY
CHRIST INVITES US OUT TO BE HIS DISCIPLES

So then let's also run the race

that is laid out in front of us, since we have such

a great cloud of witnesses surrounding us.

Let's throw off any extra baggage, get rid of the sin

that trips us up, and fix our eyes on Jesus,

faith's pioneer and perfecter. He endured the cross,

ignoring the shame, for the sake of the joy that

was laid out in front of Him, and sat down

at the right hand of God's throne.

— Hebrews 12:1-2

CHAPTER 1

BEGIN WITH "JESUS IS LORD"

*Thomas asked, 'Lord, we don't know where You are going.
How can we know the way?' Jesus answered, 'I am the way,
the truth, and the life. No one comes to the Father except
through Me.'*
(*John 14:5-6*)

*To those with eyes to see and ears to hear, Jesus Himself
is sign enough of His true identity.*
(Frederick Coutts, *The Armoury Commentary—The Four
Gospels*)

O Christ, my life, possess me utterly.
Take me and make a little Christ of me.
If I am anything but Thy Father's son,
'Tis something not yet from the darkness won.
Oh, give me light to live with open eyes.
Oh, give me life to hope above all skies.
Give me Thy spirit to haunt the Father with my cries.
(George MacDonald, *Diary of an Old Soul*)

Let's begin our journey with the Old Testament. The Torah
(first five books of the Bible) are the definitive Scriptures for
the rest of the Old Testament. All the Old Testament books
that follow are rooted in the Torah because the Torah tells
the original story of the Jews, reveals the Covenant which
defines the nature of their relationship with God, and pro-

vides the Law by which all good Jews were to live.

The Torah is summarized in **Deuteronomy 6:4-5**. It's called the *Shema*, Hebrew for "hear," the command for all of Israel to pay attention to what is to follow: "Israel, listen! Our God is the Lord! Only the Lord! Love the Lord your God with all your heart, all your being [or soul], and all your strength." This is the essence of Hebrew faith. What follows in that chapter are descriptions of how the Jews are to reinforce that faith throughout each day, remember the stories of God's faithful care of them over the years, tell their children these stories and teach them the Torah, and live out the *Shema* by their own obedience to God in observing the Torah.

For the Hebrews of the Old Testament, the key to their future was to live by this Torah, this Law. And that's why they recited the *Shema* over and over: Our only God is Yahweh, and we will love Him with all our hearts, all our being, and all our strength—and we will do it by obeying the Torah.

Do we Christians have a *Shema*? When Jesus was asked which of all the commandments was the most important, He answered by quoting the *Shema* from **Deuteronomy 6:4-5**, and then He added **Leviticus 19:18b** as part of it: "love your neighbor as yourself." (**Mark 12:29-31; Matthew 22:37-40; Luke 10:27**) So we Christians have our *Shema*. Then do we have our own Torah, as well? Phyllis Tickle suggests that the four Gospels are the Christian Torah, and if this is so, then the four Gospels spell out for us how to live out *our Shema* (*The Words of Jesus*). The way we surrender to Jesus' lordship is by loving Him completely, serving Him faithfully, and loving our neighbors as ourselves.

A radically different Lord

We Christians are Christ-centered monotheists: We believe in one God fully revealed in the incarnate Son of God, God in the flesh, Jesus the Christ (Alan Hirsch, *The Forgotten Ways*). Well, what exactly does that mean? It means "Jesus is Lord," but not in the usual way we think of "lordship." Someone is a "lord" because he or she has power over others and will not hesitate to use it to protect that power base. Jesus is Lord, however, because He has power and will not hesitate to give it up if and when the exercise of that power stands in the way of His loving us and our loving Him.

It's the apostle Paul who puts this strange monotheism into a creed, which is really a story. The story flows like poetry: The Son of God makes Himself nothing, humbles Himself into human servanthood, refuses to use His divine power for self-protection, uses it only for the saving and healing of others, and gets Himself killed for doing it. For this very reason, says Paul, His lordship of love has credibility, God exalts Him, and the whole human race is invited to confess Him as Lord (**Philippians 2:6-11**). Jesus is Lord because He gave up His power, His self-protection, His divine invulnerability... *for us!* Who ever heard of such a creed? Who ever heard of a self-emptying king?

A sold-out obedience

If this passage in Philippians were just a creed to be recited, then all we'd have to do is believe it and be happy that "Jesus paid it all," and go on as we are, assured of our undeserved salvation. What a deal!

If only it were that convenient. It's actually quite *incon-venient*. There's a reason why Paul recites this creed at this point in his letter to the Philippian church. He's doing it in order to try to get the members of this church to *act like Jesus*.

Oh, *that's* the deal! You mean humble *ourselves*, empty *ourselves*? Well, yes. As followers of Jesus, the Philippian Christians were supposed to imitate Him and manifest the same attitude and state of mind, the same self-emptying love, the same unity of spirit, the same astonishing humility. They were to pursue not their own selfish ambitions but the good of each other. To begin to obey Jesus is to begin to be like Jesus (**Philippians 2:1-5**). Our Christian *Shema* calls us not only to believe in our Lord Jesus, not only to have faith in Him and what He's done for us; our *Shema* also calls us—in fact it commands us—to *imitate* Him. To be like Him. To be disciples with a sufficient degree of credibility.

When it comes to confessing that Jesus is our Lord, the *medium* is the message, and *we are* the medium. Claiming the creed in the church is not enough. Living the creed is everything. Our lives are the only medium that truly embod-ies the message. The claim that "Jesus is Lord" has no real medium of convincing communication unless we are living it. "Hear, O Christians, Jesus is Lord, and you need to act like it and show it. You need to surrender yourself to it."

Surrender to God has always been His expectation of us, and in our obedience we have found the destiny for which we were intended. To a tongue-tied Moses the Lord says, "Go lead a holy rebellion." Who, Lord, *me*? "Yes, *you*." To an abused prophet named Jeremiah, "Go on, keep at this calling that causes you such grief." Lord, is this really necessary? "Yes, go!" To a man named Hosea, abandoned by an adulterous wife, "Go find her and bring her home." But Lord, she left me! "I know. Go anyway!"

To a young girl named Mary, "I've chosen you to have a baby, yes to get pregnant before marriage and suffer the humiliation, but don't worry, it'll be the Holy Spirit's doing." And the girl says, "Uh...okay. I am the Lord's servant. Let it be with me just as You have said."

To a tax collector named Matthew, "Leave your money bags and your fair (or unfair) cut of the taxes, and follow this man Jesus, who only offers you poverty." Give up my financial security? "Yes, all of it." Uh...okay.

To an up-and-coming Pharisee named Saul, making a reputation for himself, he was, weeding out the disciples of this renegade Jew called Jesus, "Saul, get on your knees blind, and go *join* that renegade crowd in Damascus." But Lord, that's a total reversal for me! "I know. Go!" Okay. And to a certain disciple named Ananias, who is in Damascus dreading the arrival of Pharisee Saul, ruthless persecutor of Christians, "Find Saul and lay hands on him so he can see again. He's now my chosen agent." But, Lord, he's been trying to kill us off! "I know, Ananias. Just trust Me. The guy has made a 180. He's not the same man. Go to him." And with fear and trembling, Ananias goes.

And to that unstable rock on which Jesus was planning to build His church: "Peter, get over your narrow religiosity, and go be a guest in the home of that Roman pagan Cornelius and convert him." "Lord, me, a devout Jew? You wouldn't ask me to associate with a Gentile at such close quarters, would You? Oh, You would? Okay."

These are just a handful of the myriad examples crawling all over the Bible and beyond. They all answered, "Yes – yes, because *You are Lord!*" In their obedience they discovered who *they* really were and what their lives were meant for. "Jesus is Lord" is for us far more than a creed; it's a surrender. We go where we wouldn't otherwise go, and do what we wouldn't otherwise do. And as we live out that choice, we find ourselves, our true selves – or better, we find something in us that begins to look like a soul on fire. "Jesus is Lord" is not a concept to be understood; it is a life to be lived out in obedience. It is coming out from our confined spirituality and following Jesus to a place we had not imagined.

A holy life

How do we describe this life of sold-out obedience? Salvationists call it holiness, referred to in the Tenth Article of our Doctrines as "the privilege of all believers." *All* believers. Not a privilege in the sense of being an option, as if there were two kinds of Christians: holy and unholy. Conversion was never the end game for Jesus. It's the doorway to make it possible for us to become what Jesus *really* intends: to make us His radical followers, His holy people, who live in fellowship with Him and each other, and follow Him out into the world eager to share the holy love of God with others. Holy living was *always* in the plan.

The apostle Paul tells the Ephesian church that "God's

goal is for us to become mature adults—to be fully grown, measured by the standard of the fullness of Christ." They are called to be disciples who "grow in every way into Christ," not spiritual infants who are unsteady on their feet, swayed and misled in every direction (**Ephesians 4:12-15**). Paul tells the Colossian church that the goals of his team's teaching and preaching is "so that we might present each one mature [full grown, finished, complete] in Christ" (**Colossians 1:28**). Living a holy life is to be the norm, not the exception for the church. In fact, Christ gave Himself up for the church "to make her holy" (**Ephesians 5:25-26**). Why would the church ever allow itself not to be Christ's holy Bride?

But it happened, over and over. As the early church grew and membership in the church became easier and easier, and as the bar for joining continued to be lowered, genuine holiness became rarer and rarer—so much so that the church had to develop an official process for identifying and labeling "authentic saints." And that, of course, made it increasingly difficult for the average churchgoer to believe that holiness was possible for him. But, of course, he could appeal to the merits of one of the great saints in Heaven (officially designated as such) to compensate for the deficiencies of his own meager holiness. Holiness was the norm no longer, only the exception. Few were being discipled.

This state of affairs is heresy in practice. When the church—and that includes our Salvation Army—fails to disciple converts, and to continue to disciple members themselves, in holiness and for holy living, the people of God are being denied participation in the very purpose of Jesus' mission: to make us like Him! Jesus did not come primarily to get us to confess our sins and join His church, although He knew our sins needed to be confessed and we needed the support of fellow believers. His bottom line went beyond that: He came to sanctify us and make us His credible disciples.

He came to make us holy, which is what it means to be fully, fittingly, and authentically *human!* Being "human" is not an excuse for our failures and sins, as we claim it is when we say, to excuse a failure or a sin, "I'm only human, you know." God created us as humans, we lost our true humanity when we sinned, and in Christ He restored our humanity. Being human is our true destiny! Jesus came to make us human again, to free us from our awful inhumanity! Holiness is not at odds with our true humanity. To be holy is to be complete human beings, or to be well on the way to it. Frederick Coutts describes it as a journey: "The New Testament doctrine of holiness is one of progress, not progress to Christ so much as progress in Christ—and this rule governs the whole of the way from earth to Heaven" (*The Splendor of Holiness*).

Holiness is the reclaiming of our true identity and character as that part of God's creation fashioned "in His image"—able not only to receive the love of God, but to return love, able not only to receive and enjoy the pleasure God gives us but also to give God pleasure. *That* is authentic human behavior. That is holiness. T. Henry Howard underlines the point when he says:

> Holiness is not intended to make human beings less or other than men or women by removing the faculties and powers that constitute such. No faculty or power or appetite with which nature endows itself is evil. The evil lies in their perversion. They have been used for

a wrong end, and their misuse has grown into an evil habit that conquers the better nature. They need to be renewed and restored to the God-given purpose. (*Fuel for Sacred Flame*)

We know that Jesus' death on the cross and the coming of the Spirit at Pentecost released the kind of power that makes holy living possible. But it is the life of Jesus that gives us the model to follow, and we find the story of His life in the four Gospels. Unfortunately, we sometimes see the Gospels as primarily a storybook for children. We may ignore the Gospels because we like to get into Paul's theology and have doctrinal discussions and debates. The truth is, the Gospels are the most demanding and even threatening part of the New Testament, especially for Christians who actually believe Jesus intends that we imitate Him.

Jesus, as an adult, appeared on the scene in Palestine as a rabbi or teacher. He did what rabbis of that day did: He gathered around Him people who wanted to become His disciples or followers so that He could teach them the way to live in God's sight and could be a model of this way of life His disciples could imitate. This is why we Salvationists sing such songs as "To be like Jesus, this hope possesses me, in every thought and deed, this is my aim, my creed" (John Gowans). Imitation of Jesus has been the desire of all great Christian exemplars and leaders. A disciple of Jesus is not a celebrity fan who finds his identity in his star's high profile. He is a student who is fully committed to imitating his teacher. Disciples of Jesus are those who "imitate God like dearly loved children...by following the example of Christ" (**Ephesians 5:1-2**).

We read the Gospels, first, so that we can learn about Jesus and, second, so that we can imitate our Rabbi Lord. And we read each other. What do I mean by that? Well, we can read about Jesus, but where can we see Jesus today? Where do we see living examples of Jesus? Well, since we're imitators of Jesus, we're all "little Jesuses" if you like, or we're supposed to be. According to **Acts 11:26**, the followers of Jesus were first called "Christians" in Antioch. The word in the Greek New Testament is *Christianous*, meaning "Little Christs." The Antiocheans used the word as a term of derision: "Ha, ha, look at those 'little Christs,' trying to imitate this Jesus of Nazareth!" Their joking actually got it right. The Antiochian Christians were drawn both to the holiness of Jesus' life and to His call to make it a way of life for themselves—everywhere.

Holiness is *being* like Jesus. Discipleship is *acting* like Jesus. You can't really have one without the other. Furthermore, we need to be Jesus to one another. Each of us needs to have enough of Jesus in us to provide something worth imitating. More than once in his letters, Paul invites his readers to imitate his apostolic team (See, for example, **Galatians 4:12; Philippians 4:8-9; I Thessalonians 1:6-7**). If anything keeps us on our toes, it's this calling to be "little Christs." How are people to see Jesus if they don't see Him in us? The medium *is* the message.

A missional family

Where does our corps congregation fit into this calling? Well, the corps is our spiritual family, isn't it? What do good Jesus-families do? They encourage each other (**Hebrews**

10:25). They build each other up **(Ephesians 4:12)**. They help one another to become "fully grown, measured by the standard of the fullness of Christ" **(4:14-16)**. They teach each other the family culture, the culture of holiness. They instill the family DNA, the DNA of Christ. They learn to live by the values of the Kingdom of God that Jesus taught and modeled (see, for example, **Matthew 5-7**). They worship and pray together, share bread and miracles, teach each other, get along together, and allow no family members to be in need **(Acts 2:42-47)**. Our corps congregation is called to be that kind of family!

John's Gospel records Jesus praying that His disciples together become *one*, just as He and the Father are one. He then goes on to say that this unity, this genuine intimacy within the Body of Christ, isn't just for our own benefit and pleasure. It's so that "the world will know that [the Father] sent [the Son]" **(John 17:20-23)**. In other words, when the Father's love for the Son has been richly shared within our corps itself, bringing members together in a holy love relationship, a unity is created that bears testimony to the world of God's transforming love. No wonder when those first Christians in Jerusalem displayed this family love, three thousand people decided to join! **(Acts 2:41)** Our very unity as a corps is a powerful evangelical witness. "See how those Christians love one another" is what the pagan Mediterranean world used to say.

Let us not be mistaken, however. All our encouraging and building up, all our nurturing of one another, all our discipling, all our mutual help, all our sharing with one another, all our inspired worship and fervent prayer—all of it can turn sour if we confine it to the corps congregation. Salt concentrated in one large lump is bitter; salt scattered draws the flavor of the kingdom Jesus is calling us to help Him usher in. What Jesus intends is that what happens in our corps prepares us for our mission. The church of Jesus exists not for itself, but for its mission in the world. The call of our resurrected Lord is for us, all of us, to go and make disciples. Our corps is a launching pad for mission. The mission field is where we let our light shine and ultimately prove that "Jesus is Lord" (**Matthew 5:13-16; 28:16-20; I Corinthians 1:21-25**).

The mission of our corps and of every Salvationist is to live out our holiness in the world. This holiness lived out speaks, even to the most spiritually lost soul, of someone he can be if he were his true self. Jesus caused a stir wherever He was because people suspected He knew who they were meant to be, and it either scared them into resisting Him, or it drew them to follow Him. We are all called to be His Christians (His "little Christs") in the world. As imperfectly as we may reflect Jesus, the Holy Spirit will work even through our inadequacies to give people a glimpse of something for which they long, a hint of who they were meant to be. We plant Gospel seeds and nurture Gospel crops every day, and God gives increases for His Kingdom. Sometimes we are privileged to see the outcome of our Jesus-like living, sometimes not. What is important is that, with Holy Spirit courage, we are living in the world in a kingdom-of-God way, following our Lord Jesus as closely as we know. And it begins when we open the door of our lives and our corps to discover Christ in His God-so-loved world—and follow Him outside.

FOR REFLECTION & PRAYER

What Scripture verse or passage in this chapter spoke most deeply to you, or challenged you most? Say why.

A radically different Lord

Personal: As a disciple of a self-emptying Lord, what is your biggest current challenge in following Him? Specifically, what is the Holy Spirit inviting you to empty yourself of in order better to follow Him?

Your corps: What do you think it would be worth your corps congregation giving up in order better to help them pursue their calling?

A sold-out obedience

Personal: What new step toward a more inconvenient but positive obedience might the Holy Spirit be leading you to take at this time?

Your corps: Is there a positive decision or step your corps might take to do something concrete together in obedience to their Lord Jesus?

A holy life

Personal: Have you made a decision to pursue holiness (being like Jesus) full measure? If not, what would you need to do to free yourself to make that decision?

Your corps: What step(s) could you personally take to help your corps better to cultivate a congregation of Salvationists who are "little Christs" **to each other**?

A missional family

Personal: Do you see your whole life as a participation in Christ's mission in the world? Is there a specific decision or step the Holy Spirit is inviting you to take as a witnessing disciple in the world in which you live?

Your corps: What step(s) could your corps take better to prepare corps members to live as "little Christs" **in the world**? Who could you talk to about this?

CHAPTER 2

PURSUE HOLINESS FULL MEASURE

Fill Thou my life, O Lord my God,
In every part with praise,
That my whole being may proclaim
Thy being and Thy ways.
Not for the lip of praise alone,
Nor e'en the praising heart
I ask, but for a life made up
Of praise in every part!

So shall each fear, each fret, each care
Be turned into a song,
And every winding of the way
The echo shall prolong;
So shall no part of day or night
From sacredness be free;
But all my life, in every step,
Be fellowship with Thee.
(Horatius Bonar, *TSSB*, 361, vv. 1,4)

In many lands the churches have literally stolen Christ
from the people; they have taken Christianity from the
city and imprisoned it behind altar rails.
(Henry Drummond, *The City Without a Church*)

Jesus preached to crowds comprised mostly of common
people whose lives were so dominated by keeping food on the

table and clothing on their family's backs, they had little time or energy to pursue the rites and observe the laws of holy living demanded by their Jewish religion. The complicated commands of the sacred traditions were hard to figure out, much less to observe. Many in the crowds were the crippled and disabled. And then there were those who lived in a way that publicly defied the ethical norms of the religious establishment—they were called publicans, tax collectors, and prostitutes. Quite a crowd Jesus gathered!

Amazingly, these were the folks in whom Jesus placed the most hope. The signs that He was the awaited Messiah were that the poor had the Gospel preached to them, prisoners were released, the blind received sight, and the oppressed were liberated (**Luke 4:18**). The healing of the sick and crippled were signs that the Kingdom of God had arrived (**Matthew 10:7-8; 12:28**). The feeding of the hungry crowd was a sign Jesus was the awaited one (**John 6:1-15**). Conversely, the person who had more than enough to eat and who hoarded his wealth would find it extremely difficult to enter the kingdom Jesus preached—as difficult as it would be for a camel to walk through the eye of a needle! (**Mark 10:25; Luke 12:15-21**). And here's the real shocker: The tax collectors and prostitutes who believed in Jesus would enter the Kingdom of God before many of the religious leaders of that day (**Matthew 21:31-32**).

The Kingdom of God Jesus preached was open to those who believed in Him. It was closed to those whose confidence and security were in their privileged religious practice or their material wealth. Generally, the marginalized, who had little else to trust in, were in a better position to trust Jesus. The door was opened wide to those who brought nothing in their hands, save faith.

This did not mean, however, that the marginalized responders to the Gospel message were given cheap passage to eternal rewards. God's love for the worst of sinners is not paternal indulgence. The least schooled in the religious life are not to be pitied. They are to be loved into a relationship with Christ leading to a changed life.

The New Testament is brimming with transformation. The prodigal son did not come back to a life of indulgence at home; he came back to receive—by grace this time—his forfeited status of sonship and to start *living* as a son (**Luke 15:11-32**). The adulterous woman was not forgiven by Jesus in order that she might continue in adultery without guilt; she was forgiven so that she could start a totally new and different life (**John 8:3-11**). Paul, the "chief of sinners," was not justified by grace only to fall irresistibly back into the sin of spiritual legalism; he was justified so that, never again having to strive for God's acceptance, he could be free (**Galatians 5:1**).

Our early Army records are replete with one account after another of miraculous transformation. The real "trophies of grace" were not those of the people who confessed their sins but went no further with Christ; they were those who did about-faces and pursued sanctifying grace. They were mostly rough sorts and social dregs. Newspaperman W.T. Stead reported on the results of one of the early Army revivals:

> The odd, miraculous thing that bothered [the town of] Darlington was that all the riff-raff of the town went to Livingston Hall, and many of them did not return home the same men. (Robert Sandall, *The History of The Salvation Army*, London:

Thomas Nelson and Sons, Ltd., vol. 2, p. 9)

Many of the transformed, well known locally as "notorious sinners," became "prominent daily witnesses for Christ" ("The Christian Mission... As a Salvation Army," pamphlet, n.d., p. 3). These were living miracles, more than heat-of-the-moment conversions. They were common people becoming uncommon saints, the fallen becoming followers, the unholy now embracing holy living.

The Salvation Army, with roots in the Wesleyan holiness revival, has been a part of what is called the Holiness Movement from the time of its beginnings. Over the years the Movement, eager to maintain its tradition, seems, however, to have lost a good bit of its traction. The signs of a holy life have often been reduced to such things as conservative styles of dress and outmoded hair styles, as holiness churches and denominations have chosen to withdraw from the world in protected enclaves of holy practices. The obvious result has been a constricted understanding of holy living and an unfortunate reduction of influence precisely in the place where holy living is most desperately needed: the world!

Our Army has a tradition of holy engagement in the world. We might call it "worldly holiness," not in any sense that true holiness is compromised, but in the sense that true holiness is compassionate. True holiness is suffocated by confinement. It simply must be lived out and proven on the real battlefields of life. That is our Army's real holiness tradition. It is the tradition that sees Christ outside the corps' doors, beckoning us to immerse ourselves and our holiness in the world as a leavening influence for the Kingdom of God.

We Salvationists must ask ourselves if we are guarding our tradition of worldly holiness and following our calling to live out that tradition in practical and compassionate ways. We must ask if we are moving in the direction of a separation between our spiritual and our social work, our corps life and our life in the world, our holy practices (increasingly confined?) and our secular practices (increasingly expanding?).

To address these questions, we must begin with an overall understanding of what Jesus' life and ministry teach us about holiness. In this chapter we will not so much get into specifics as paint with a broad brush. We will talk about three major dimensions of holy living which, if we understand them and seek to live them out, we will be in a good position from which to deal with more specific and concrete questions of Christian living. In our understanding of holiness, there are three things it is essential we get right: 1) Holiness is an intimate relationship, not a set of rules. 2) Holiness is a way of life, not a part of life. 3) Holiness is a calling out, not a settling in. Let's explore them.

An intimate relationship, not a set of rules

Holiness is not a conscious rectitude, a continual watching of one's step lest the wrong foot be put forward first. Separation, by itself, is not enough. Holiness is not just doing things and not going places. I am not made good by what I do not do. (The Privilege of All Believers)

I grew up in the religious environment of a Salvationist family. There were certain rules of Christian practice, and my siblings and I were expected to live by them. There were the Sunday meetings and other corps activities during the week. We had family devotions and said our prayers before going to bed. Conversation at home was to be civil, and denigration of other people was frowned upon. These were some of the religious laws we lived by, and they were good for us. Our Christian faith must be lived out in some disciplined way.

I did think that some Christians went too far. When I was twelve years of age, a revivalist came to the corps where my parents were corps officers and stayed in our home during the week of meetings. I was chagrined to learn that he believed TV exposed Christians to too much temptation, so our parents, in deference to our guest, decided we would not have the TV on all week—meaning for me, no Lone Ranger episode for that week. I also remember the revivalist raising his hand in Sunday School and saying, "This is a hand that has never spent a nickel on a movie." It just so happened in those days my neighborhood friend and I went to the neighborhood theater most Saturday afternoons to see a cowboy movie and a couple of cartoons—yes, for a nickel. Was something wrong with me that I felt no guilt? I concluded the revivalist lived on a higher plane of spirituality reserved only for the hardy few. After all, he drank this disgusting thing called buttermilk—surely a suffering only the spiritually elite could endure, and I was determined I would never be able to do that!

As a child I was becoming aware that different Christians practiced different laws. When it came to matters like TV, movies, and buttermilk, I wasn't sure where the commands of God came from and why different Christians had different views on such matters. Once I entered adulthood I had become aware that the dos and don'ts of Christian practice could vary considerably from one Christian and Christian group to another. But the worst thing was that they were frequently also the occasions for smugness, infighting, and division within the whole spectrum of Christianity—clearly not good for the overall health of the Body of Christ and the claim of all Christians to be following the very same Lord and Rabbi.

It's a real temptation for us to reduce holy living to a set of rules, maybe especially since we're an Army. Armies have to be run by rules, don't they? Of course, and every denomination has its rules, customs, and membership expectations. They're not all sacred, but sometimes we act as if they were. There was a time when every soldier was expected to wear the uniform, and the assumption was that if he or she showed up without it, well, there must be something wrong spiritually. Really? Well, what about the possibility of a soldier, or an officer, using the uniform to camouflage a sinful heart or an otherwise unholy lifestyle? And have you ever met a uniform-wearing Salvationist with a heart of stone? What about the possibility of my obeying all the rules of behavior as a "good Salvationist," finding my comfortable place in the corps community, maybe in a leadership position—all the while my relationship with the Lord may be weakening, even as I go through the motions of a good soldier, or officer.

Holy living is not about uniforms, though I wear mine proudly because of what it stands for. Holy living is not about rules, though the holy life cannot be lived without disciplines and behaviors that make it concrete. Holy living is not about wearing ourselves out to prove our holiness, though a true holiness always bears rich fruit for the Kingdom of God, some of it, sometimes most of it, immeasurable by our statistical printouts.

Holiness is *an intimate relationship*. It begins with the intimacy of the Trinity—Father, Son, and Holy Spirit in perfect relationship. We can especially thank John's Gospel for giving us a view into Jesus' own intimacy with the Father. His prayer times were inviolate rendezvous with the Father, an intimacy so deep He described it as He and the Father dwelling in each other (**John 14:10**), an unbreakable oneness (**10:30**). So deep was the relationship, when we look at Jesus we actually see the Father (**14:9**). And the good news for us is that Jesus shares the love He receives from the Father with us (**15:9**). Jesus, the Beloved of the Father, invites *us* to become the Father's beloved (**14:21**) by loving Jesus. Spending time with Him, walking with Him throughout our day, imbibing His holiness, loving Him.

"Simon, son of John, do you love Me more than these?" Three times Peter answers with a broken heart and voice, "Yes, Lord, You know that I love You." Then feed My lambs, take care of My sheep, and again, feed My lambs. Follow Me, not your fond set of rules. Peter was a rules guy, and it took him time to get past his religion of rules—for example, the rule that Jewish Christians shouldn't violate the law of Jews not sitting down with Gentiles for supper. Diligent Peter, trying so hard to get it right with the rules, too often missing the relationship. Rules are helpful, except when they get in the way of following Jesus (**John 21:15-17**).

The more we live out our Christian faith by the rules, the more we tend to compare ourselves to other Christians. We see this in what follows in Peter's encounter with his resurrected Lord—immediately following this moving exchange! Peter suddenly releases this moment of intimacy like a burning coal, and deflects the pain of his failure to a fellow disciple: "Lord, what about him?" Jesus must be heartbroken at His beloved Peter's turning away, as if the other disciple's place in Jesus' plan should matter to Peter's relationship with his Lord. Peter was not yet ready to give up his rules-based, comparing righteousness, his drive to be Jesus' prize pupil in the class of disciples (**21:20-22**).

Our resurrected Lord is not a distant sovereign issuing orders to us His minions. He's the Divine Lover who wants to share life with us. In John's Gospel we get a very strong sense of this close intimacy between Jesus and His disciples (see, for example, **John 14:1-3; 15:1-5a; 17:25-26**). And just before His departure and ascent to the Father, He tells them, "And surely I am *with you always*, to the very end of the age" (**Matthew 28:20**, italics added). The apostle Paul sees Christ Jesus as God bridging the separation between us and God and giving us the sweeping victory of a love from which nothing, absolutely nothing can separate us (**Romans 8:35-38**). "We will always be with the Lord," he says (**I Thessalonians 4:17b**). An eternal intimacy with God in Christ, through the Spirit.

Intimacy is the whole point. God longs for a relationship with us humans. He created us "in His image" precisely so that He could have this loving relationship with us through eternity. Since "your life is hidden with Christ in God," says the apostle Paul, "when Christ, who is your life, is revealed, then you also will be revealed with Him in glory" (**Colossians 3:3-4***)*. That's why Jesus assured His disciples that one day they would be reunited (**John 14:1-3**). Not only that, during the interim, for however long it takes for His return, He will be present with them through the Holy Spirit, who will keep the remembrance of Jesus alive (**John 4:25-26; 15:26**). In fact, the Holy Spirit will re-present Jesus to them (**John 16:12-16**).

There is in all of us a longing for God. We're just not complete without Him. We're made and molded to be in close relationship with Father, Son, and Holy Spirit. True, some are more in touch with that deep longing than others. Some claim they don't need God, or have no awareness they do. Others are very aware of their God-longing – like the psalmist who cries out, "Whom have I in Heaven but You? there is nothing on earth I desire more than You" (**Psalm 73:25**, NRSV).

Holiness is an intimate relationship with Jesus. In **Mark 3:13-15** Jesus calls His disciples *first* "to be with Him," and *then* "to be sent out to preach and to have authority to throw out demons." If we try to do our Lord's bidding without the abiding, we're on a fool's mission. I've found that out through experience, and I dare say you may have, as well. Christ does not stand at the door knocking to send us out on our own with a "good luck" from Him. He sends us out in His own company, always with us, never forsaking us (**Matthew 28:20b**).

Like Peter, we Christians, all of us, are called first to be with Jesus. He is right next to us, loving us, teaching us, pointing out the way for us. It is not enough for Him that He has our allegiance; He wants our closeness so that we can begin to have His likeness. Holiness is intimacy with our Lord as we live our lives in the world. Holiness is also

A way of life, not a part of life

The early Salvationists understood that coming to faith in Jesus meant all of their lives had to change. They were not saved to come to church; they were saved to live all day as disciples of Jesus. Converts were checked out to make sure they were living their faith 24/7. The more informal, sometimes even rowdy character of the religious meetings, and the adoption of a culture well suited to working-class life, not only made the target population more at home, it also helped them better to connect their newfound faith with the life they lived outside the meetings. They didn't have to assume a culturally false self at the Army. They could be themselves.

The churches that were scandalized by the Army's boisterous worship seemed blinded by their own social prejudices. One Christian newspaper accused the Army of "utterly vulgarizing the holiest things" (Quoted in Sandall, II, p. 163). Salvationists believed the opposite: They were sanctifying the most common things. They may well have taken their cue from the apostle Paul's words about God choosing the world's foolish to shame the wise, the world's weak to shame the strong, the world's nothings to shame the somethings (**I Corinthians 1:27-31**). The Gospel would not succeed with the marginalized by getting them into churches that sang tunes they didn't know or like, that spoke a form of English they couldn't speak, that confessed creeds they couldn't understand, that behaved in ways that made them feel totally out of place—and that consigned them to crude, wooden benches in the back because they couldn't afford to rent pews. These churches could not relate to the world of those who, in Victorian England, were most like the poor crowds that Jesus spent most of His time with. Jesus did not expect any of them to become like the highly religious practitioners of Judaism. He only asked that they follow and obey Him.

Our relationship with Jesus amounts to little if it is confined to our experience in a church culture that is not carried over into our common life in the world. Christian faith must go public, or it shrivels into empty ritual. It must be strengthened and proven on the battlefield of every day. Jesus' call to discipleship is always a "Follow Me." And we do it in two ways: by communing with Jesus (that's the intimacy) and by living His life everywhere (that's the imitation). In the intimacy our Lord works to make our corrupted hearts whole. In the imitation He sends us to be tested and tried, to succeed and fail, to learn and unlearn, as we improve and begin actually to get it, to understand how to "be like Jesus" in real life—to be pilgrims in His company every day, life travelers with God. "Happy are the people," says the psalmist, "whose hearts are set on the pilgrim way" (**Psalm 84:5**).

The words of our resurrected Lord to a Peter who had quickly gotten distracted must be heard over and over by every one of us. "You must follow *Me!*" Don't let anything distract you from that. Follow Jesus, imitate Jesus, be Jesus to each other and to the world. Yes, holiness is a personal experience where through the Holy Spirit we develop a deep relationship with Jesus, who unites us with the Father. But we cannot safely secure this relationship in a kind of holy isolation. "For *their* sakes I sanctify Myself," said Jesus. And He says to us: "You are the light of the world [every one of you who are My disciples].... Let your light shine before people, so they can see the good things you do and praise your Father who is in Heaven" (**Matthew 5:14, 16**, italics added). Go public!

Holiness is a total way of life. It isn't a spiritual status to worry about, or fight about, or brag about. It isn't about something we attain, an acquisition we can then permanently pocket, an achievement we can then add to our spiritual trophies. It's a personal relationship with Jesus that goes public. We live it out in every relationship—our friends, family, fellow Salvationists, neighbors, fellow workers and business associates, our enemies, the whole world. We really are candles of the Lord in a world longing for the light of God's love. Holiness is a total way of life.

So, what does going public look like? Parading our spirituality like a fanfare? Jesus says "No." He says, follow Me where I take you, do what I tell you, love the way I showed you. Our relationship with Jesus must transform every relationship in our lives.

Sometimes we dwell too much on the experience of holiness, while failing to address the rubber-meets-the-road realities of how to live it out in specific circumstances and relationships. How often do we have concrete conversations and hear practical sermons on, say, how we can love our enemies as Jesus did? Or how to love like Jesus in any of the situations or relationships in which we find ourselves? Wesley's words to a serious follower of Jesus are worth hearing. The man was doing his best to live the holy life, but he was somewhat depressed because he didn't feel he had *experienced* entire sanctification. In response Wesley didn't outline steps to the experience for him; he simply said, "Love the Lord and live the life He taught us to live, and the Lord will see to the experience in His own way."

Jesus preached and modeled a rubber-meets-the-road holiness. He taught neither proper religious behavior nor theological concepts; He taught a way of life. He was a rabbi. He appeared on the scene and did what rabbis of that day did: He gathered around Him disciples who studied the way of living He taught and modeled. Why did He, the Savior of the human race, spend so much of His time teaching us how to live as His disciples? He did it to show us the life for which we are saved. He did it to teach us how the holiness He makes possible can actually be lived day by day. He did it so that we can find the freedom of obeying Him. That wonderful saint of the 19th Century, George MacDonald, tells us very plainly what it means to follow our Rabbi Jesus:

> It is simply absurd to say that you believe, or even want to believe in [Jesus], if you do not [do] anything He tells you.... But you can begin at once to be a disciple of the Living One—by obeying Him in the first things you can think of in which you are not obeying Him. We must learn to obey Him in everything, and so must begin somewhere. Let it be at once, and in the very next thing that lies at the door of our conscience! Oh, fools and slow of heart, if you think of nothing but Christ, and do not set yourselves to do His words, you but build your houses on the sands (*Creation in Christ*).

Christ stands outside the door of our compartmentalized Christianity, inviting us to follow Him and live for Him in every way, place, and time of our lives. Holiness is a total way of life, lived in obedience to our Lord Jesus, come what may.

Finally, holiness is

A calling out, not a settling in

A life of settling never works for God's people. A corps of Salvationists that have no vital mission in the world is a corps not following Jesus. If a corps settles in behind closed doors, its holiness turns stale, its spiritual life turns bitter, and sooner or later it dies. Holiness, like love, is nurtured by giving itself on the front lines of the world. In one of His prayers to the Father, Jesus says He is sending His disciples into the world as the Father sent Him; and He is sanctifying them for this mission so that the world will see Jesus as the One sent by God and themselves as those who have received the love of God (see **John 17:15-23**). Holiness on the front lines: the real proving ground.

The very heart of the Gospel is that "The Word [the Son of God] became flesh and made His home among us" (**John 1:14a**). The story begins with God becoming a human, and the whole life of Jesus is the day-to-day roll-out of this incarnation (enfleshment). In Jesus (God fully revealed in man) we are now able to see the true glory of God (**1:14b**) and encounter the love of God reaching out to the whole world (**3:16-17**). This outward reach God, this God on the front lines of human life, is the incarnating God to which the Gospel bears testimony.

Followers of Jesus are called to be a part of this same incarnational movement of God in Jesus. Jesus fully entered our common life. He was, says the writer to the Hebrews, "made like His brothers and sisters in every way.... [and because of this He was] able to help those who are being tempted, since He Himself experienced suffering when He was tempted" (**Hebrews 2:17-18**). As His followers and imitators, we also are called to leave our secure places and venture out into the lives of others, humbling ourselves like Jesus so that we can actually begin to understand them and love them genuinely. So that we can in some way, however imperfectly, be Jesus to them. Little Christs.

The Salvation Army came into being as an evangelistic movement. The initial intention of converts being referred to churches for membership and further discipling, however, proved unworkable. Most of the converts found their way back to the Army, enlarging the ranks considerably. The Army became a spiritual home, a church, for its own converts. It now had the personnel to expand rapidly around the world, and it did. It did because Salvationists incarnated themselves into the lives of others.

Fast forward to the present, and we find a number of corps, especially in the Western world, that have settled in well but are minimizing or even avoiding the calling-out. Some corps faithfully celebrate a Salvationist church culture as their religious identity, while failing to practice the evangelical outreach that is at the heart of that culture. A few corps work hard to downplay our unique Salvationist identity so as to become more respectable and look like other churches. Are we retreating from incarnational living, from the road less traveled taken by Jesus?

Consider the meaning of the Greek word that's used in the New Testament to describe the people of God, the word we translate as "church." It's a word that literally means "called out." That's who we Christians are, the called-out people of God. Yes, we are the church when we gather for worship, when we open our church doors to anyone, when what takes place at the corps ministers to our needs, heals our wounds, and helps us grow saints. But we are *most* the church outside our doors, when we are like scattered grains of salt, releasing the flavor of Jesus, each of us, wherever we are. And we are certainly most like a movement called The Salvation Army... out there!

Alan Hirsch says that Jesus didn't found a church as we think of "church" today. He founded a *movement*. A movement that gathers in order to be scattered like seeds, or salt, or a holy virus infecting the population with Jesus (*The Forgotten Ways*).

By definition, a movement invests most of its time and energy for those who are not in the movement. William and Catherine Booth, and their beginning Army, founded a movement whose focus and obsession was a sea of drowning and desperate humanity.

The world will get saved by Christian movements, not walled churches. If non-Christians just stay away from church, and Christians lay low outside the church, then non-Christians are safe—they won't get infected. And the possibility that they will show up at a church is very small, either because what they know about church is what they see on television (need I say more?), or more probably, because they have experienced enough Christians as graceless and highly judgmental. The world's salvation largely depends on how you and I live *all the time*, the kind of holy risks we take, and how humbly we allow the love and grace of our Lord Jesus Christ to rule our actions— out there! Nothing will open a person to the Gospel as much as in-the-world Christians looking enough like Jesus to make people curious and interested. Worldly holiness.

The Jesus we worship in our corps is the same Jesus who calls us out into the world *to find Him*. Yes, find Him! He's already there. In the words of an Isaac Watts hymn, "And everywhere that man can be, Thou, God, art present there." I'm sure He wants us to look for Him. And with the Spirit's help we will find Him, one way or another. And then, He'd probably like some help from us.

The apostle Paul found Him in every race and ethnicity he encountered in his travels across the Mediterranean world.

William and Catherine Booth and company found Him in the slums of London, and then the slums of the world.

William Noble, MD found Him in hospitals and clinics of India; Dorothy Jones in children's homes of India.

Magna Trochme, a French Protestant housewife, found Him in the face of a Jewish refugee fleeing Holocaust, who knocked on Magna's front door one day, and Magna and husband Andre hid this refugee for the remainder of the war, setting an example for fellow Christians in town, who joined the conspiracy of compassion and hid every Jew who sought safety with them.

Today Sunshine Meeks finds Him among the one hundred school children she teaches five days a week.

Today Lebron Lyons, gate attendant supervisor at a large condominium development, finds Him among the hundreds of people he greets and helps every day.

Today Ed Laity finds Him among the wide range of people he comes in contact with as president of an international fundraising consultancy.

Where in your world will you find Him? Where in their world will your corps, your fellow Salvationists, find Him? Jesus knocks at the door of our corps and asks each of us, Where will you find Me in the course of your day?

And then what will you do? How will you respond?

FOR REFLECTION & PRAYER

What Scripture verse or passage spoke most deeply to you, or challenged you most? Say why.

An intimate relationship, not a set of rules

Personal: How would you describe the level of your intimacy with Jesus? What specific step(s) could you take to spend more time with Him?

Your corps: How could your corps find ways, as groups, to get to know Jesus by spending time with Him together, as did those first twelve disciples?

A way of life, not a part of life

Personal: In what part of your day or week are you most likely to forget who you are as a follower and imitator of Jesus? How specifically might you become more like Jesus in that setting?

Your corps: What might your corps do to help you live the life of Jesus in the specific situations and challenges you have in your life outside the corps?

A calling out, not a settling in

Personal: Think of a place you spend time or a situation you face during the week where you suspect Jesus might be waiting for you to find Him present, even to be Him in some way. What do you think, or know, He is asking you to do?

Your corps: How might your corps help you see the world, not as a place where Jesus is absent, but as a place where Jesus is everywhere present, calling on His followers to join Him there and help Him extend His Kingdom?

CHAPTER 3

BE DISCIPLES

God, seeking to work in a person who offers no disciplined cooperation, is a heartbreaking spectacle—a defeated Savior trying to free, from sins and earthiness, a person who will not lift his or her face out of the dust, or shake off the shackles of the ego-centric self... We must recover for ourselves the significance and the necessity of the spiritual disciplines. Without them we shall continue to be impotent witnesses for Christ. Without them Christ will be impotent in His efforts to use us to save our society from disintegration and death.

(Albert Edward Day, *Discipline and Discovery*)

Love so amazing, so divine, demands my soul, my life, my all.
(Isaac Watts, *When I survey the wondrous cross*, SASB, v. 4)

We now come back to the all-important matter of discipleship. We've already looked at how radical discipleship was originally the expectation and even the norm for the Christian church in the beginning years. Christians were expected to follow Jesus' teachings and imitate His life. Complacency began to set in, however, when Christianity became the state religion of the Roman Empire and Roman citizenship along with infant baptism automatically implied a person's status as a Christian. Few saw the need actually to follow Jesus, especially when doing so interfered with commonly accepted cultural norms and practices. Christianity became a status rather than a calling; discipleship declined. Over the centuries various Christian movements emerged to recall the church to Jesus' radical way of living, but some, if not most, of these movements cooled off and became settled churches. Others became clipped-wings branches of an established denomination, or simply ceased to exist.

Our early Salvation Army was a radical Christian movement. We called people—in particular the marginalized—to saving faith, radical discipleship, and holy living. Will we now settle down into complacency, in whatever form that may take? Have we done so already? Perhaps we will become another institutionalized church, content to live out our unusual Salvationist culture in increasing isolation from the world around us. Or we could become a Christian social service agency delivering a high level of professional services, while downplaying our faith base and certainly any intention to share ministry and help clients seeking help with their spiritual journey. Or we could simply accept our decline and eventually cease to exist, as if a limited life span were inevitable.

These are not our only options. The call to be credible disciples of Jesus is an invitation extended to every Salvationist. A corps, as dry and as dull as it may have become, can through the Holy Spirit's ignition and direction discover God's future **(Ezekiel 37:1-14; Revelation 3:14-22)**. There are ways we Salvationists can regain our character as a vital movement of compassionate and committed disciples of Jesus. It is already happening in some places.

In order to see how Salvationists and corps as a whole

that have become complacent can become radical disciples of Jesus, we must first understand the challenges we face. What is standing in our way?

Barriers to discipleship

As strange as it may seem, there are aspects of today's church, including our Army, that work against our calling to the radical holiness of a disciple of Jesus. Consider them:

First, there is a *doctrinal problem*. It has to do specifically with our understanding of the person of Jesus. In doctrinal or theological terms, we call this Christology. The fourth article of our Eleven Doctrines states: "We believe that in the person of Jesus Christ the Divine and human natures are united, so that He is truly and properly God and truly and properly man." Jesus, the Christ, in other words, is fully God and fully man. He is not God disguised as a man, and He is not man parading as a god. He is both God and man, fully and completely.

Many Christians have difficulty accepting that Jesus really *was* a human like us, living with our limitations, tempted as we are. They see Jesus as somehow above it all. Indeed, He was a perfect human, in that sense not like us imperfect humans. But He was not permanently immune to sin—otherwise how could there be any credibility whatsoever to the claim in **Hebrews 4:15** that He really was "*tempted in every way that we are*, except without sin" (italics added)? How could He be our high priest (a human) who can "sympathize with our weaknesses," unless "He himself experienced suffering when He was tempted" **(2:18)**, as all high priests must? As crucial as Jesus' divinity is to our Christian faith, equally crucial is His humanity.

This affirmation is important to our faith for many reasons. The reason we are interested in now is Jesus' calling as our Rabbi. He appeared on the scene as a rabbi who, like other rabbis of that day, taught a way of life to the disciples He gathered around Him. He called this new way of life the Kingdom of God, and being His disciples meant entering this Kingdom through Him and living in it as His disciples or followers. He was not God disguised as a human, teaching His students a holy but impossible way to live. He was a human teaching and showing other humans how they actually *can* live, and by doing so become who they were meant to be as humans created in God's image (**Genesis 1:27; Ephesians 4:17-24; Colossians 3:8-11**).

When we ignore the human Jesus, the Rabbi who came to show us how to live as God intended, we withdraw from our calling as His disciples, even if we do it unintentionally. Instead, we may pursue a less concrete holiness, a holiness that is experiential but not grounded in real life. We may gauge our Christian experience by our spiritual highs, our personal blessings, our affirmation from other Christians. We may seek the blessing or experience of holiness without the sacrifice. In doing so we may distance ourselves from the Jesus of the Gospels, who taught us to risk and lose ourselves for His and the Gospel's sake, as the only way to save our own lives (**Mark 8:35b**). To be sure, Jesus came to save us by His death on the Cross. The apostle Paul teaches us that Jesus' death is also an invitation for us to die with Him so that we can live in His presence (**Romans 6:8**). He came as a human, one of us, to show us how to die to ourselves so that we can *live* by imitating Him. By being His disciples. Without the living, the whole point of the saving Cross is lost. And without discipleship, holiness is a sham.

The first step in taking our calling as disciples seriously is taking the humanity of Jesus seriously (**I John 4:1-3; II John 7**). If He was fully human, then He is our model for living a holy life. And if He is our model, we'd best take the Gospels seriously, where we learn how He lived and loved, where we can sit at His feet and learn, and where we can be His traveling companions on a journey so strange and stimulating it changes our whole perspective—and our lives.

And this *brings us to* another barrier to discipleship: *Our obsession with doctrinal debates and controversies.* Our doctrines are important; we must strive to be faithful to the core beliefs of Scripture. Heresies can lead us astray and must be challenged. It is laughable, however, to see Christians fighting over fine points of doctrine that in the end don't really matter. Bitter warfare has been fought over doctrinal minutia. One group defines itself over against another based on such matters as millennial interpretations or sacraments. Having a reason for the hope that is within us (**I Peter 3:15**) is one thing, obsession with intellectual matters not central to our faith is another (**I Corinthians 1:21-25**).

The outcome of this preoccupation with doctrinal minutia is the illusion that our faith is defined by doctrinal correctness. The fact is that we will share eternity not only with God and those who share our own doctrinal formulations, but also with others who have also surrendered to the lordship of Jesus and do *not* share all of our doctrinal formulations. Many Wesleyans and Calvinists will sit together at the Kingdom table. All those who are saved by grace and have become disciples of the Lord Jesus are included in the family. Preoccupation with doctrinal correctness can lure us away from the real Christian calling: living the life of Jesus in the world.

Another barrier to discipleship are *the ways we tame Jesus.* The Jesus of the Gospels is countercultural. He challenges the power mongers, be they religious leaders (**Matthew 23**), government officials (**John 19:8-12a**), or the wealthy (**Matthew 19:24; Luke 16:19-26**). He spends most of His time with the poor and the sick. He comforts the afflicted and afflicts the comforted. Do we really want to be imitating disciples of such a Jesus? It's certainly not a comfortable calling.

How do we make it easier on ourselves and still try to claim we're following Jesus? We tame Jesus. We make Him more likeable, or acceptable, or accommodating. We make Him an idol that embodies our cultural values rather than our Lord who calls us to radical, counter-cultural obedience. Let's consider some of the ways we do this:

- We tame Jesus when we identify Him too closely with our own nation and its values; we see Jesus as an endorser-in-full of our nation's values; our nation itself becomes holy. Disciples of Jesus are called to be genuine patriots, but not to worship their country. Of course, there is nothing wrong with loving their country, so long as they do not love it more or even as much as they love their God (Remember the film *Chariots of Fire*?). Actually, our Lord expects His disciples not only to be good citizens but also to act prophetically by criticizing their country when it is perpetrating evil and practicing injustice. What is the outcome when they do not do so? We need only look as far as Nazi Germany and Fascist Italy in the 1930s to see the result of too few Christians seeing clearly, speaking boldly, and acting courageously—and these were Christian countries! Those who stood in opposition based on their Christian belief and principles paid dearly. They tell a cautionary tale about the danger of treating Jesus as a true patriot of our country, when Scripture is clear He belongs exclusively to **the world** and is ready to stand in judgment over any nation that presumes to possess Him and any church that allows itself to nationalize Him.

- We tame Jesus when we admire and promote highly successful Christians—celebrity Christians—by having them as special guests at our events, by endorsing their books, and by treating them as model Christians for us to emulate. First of all, such practices carry the hidden and false message that if I follow Jesus He will enable **me** to become a Miss America, an NBA star, a very successful entrepreneur, or whatever kind of high profile person I long to be. Though this assumption may be unconscious, and even recognized as ridiculous when brought out in the open, it is clearly at work subconsciously: "I wish and really want to be **as successful as that person.**" Or even worse, if we recognize that we cannot be that person, we are made to feel as lesser persons, maybe even in God's eyes. Why do we not endorse and promote Christians who live out their faith in humbler, lower profile jobs, people who are more credible models for the great majority of us? By the way, these are the kind of folk Jesus chose to spend His time with. The celebrities had to seek Him out, or use the influence or power they had to get an audience. We tame Jesus when we dress Him in the clothing of our success-driven culture. We disguise the lowly Galilean as a model of the values and idolatries of our culture. It is both demeaning and absurd, and highly detrimental to an honest and true understanding of what it means to be Jesus' disciple.

* We tame Jesus when we forget, or intentionally decide, to limit our discipleship practice to what we do in or on behalf of the corps. When we do this, we live in two realities: the Salvationist world, within the corps or doing corps ministry, and the so-called secular world, where we spend most of our time. When we're in the Salvationist world we hopefully are worshiping, learning, being discipled, fellowshipping, helping newcomers feel at home, and using our spiritual gifts on behalf of the corps' ministry. When we enter the secular world, things may change for many of us. We may be guided by different values, values that often clash with our Christian values. Consumerism tempts us to seek meaning in material acquisition because this is how things are in the real world—we're all familiar with TV and internet preachers who promote an insidious prosperity gospel as if it were endorsed by the lowly Nazarene! Gaining more money by devious means may tempt us, and we may rationalize it as commonly accepted behavior in the real world. We may find ourselves in groups that participate in conversation that is shameful or demeans other people, but we fail to exempt ourselves and instead offer words of compassion and respect—after all, this is just the way it is in the real world. What does it mean for us to be in such situations *as disciples of Jesus*? What are we willing to risk? What values are we willing to live by in these kinds of settings—the values of a disciple of Jesus or the values of a disciple of the prevailing culture? Will we tame Jesus by confining Him to the safety of our corps life, or will we let Him loose in the world and suffer the personal consequences?

There are other barriers to discipleship, and for many of us there are barriers unique to us. The important thing is that each of us recognize the barriers in our own lives and find ways to remove them. Let's be clear: *Every Salvationist is called to be a disciple all the time. No exceptions!* Every morning Christ stands at the door of our lives and invites us to enter the world as His countercultural, authentic disciples. It is a fulltime calling; not a part-time job.

Every Salvationist a disciple

We cannot take our calling as disciples for granted. We do not automatically become and remain as disciples. To use Jesus' metaphor again, we are branches of the vine. As branches of the true vine (Jesus) we must constantly grow and produce fruit, or eventually be pruned off the vine ourselves. Growth as a branch (disciple) is essential. The word Jesus uses for this connection with Him is "remain," which in the case of a vine and its branches means continual *growth*, not the maintaining of some permanent status. No growth through Christ, no remaining in Christ (**John 15:1-8**). Like all Christians, Salvationists are called to be living branches of the vine, disciples who live in the love of and for God and each other (**vv. 9-17**).

Every corps needs to ask itself: Are we cultivating healthy branches? Are we discipling Salvationists? In what ways are we teaching and modeling the life of a disciple? In what ways are we helping our corps members remain in the vital, life-giving, forward-growing life of the Vine? How do we help them deal with the barriers to discipleship we've just discussed, or other barriers that may be specific to individual members?

How are we equipping and helping each other actually live the life of Jesus in the world?

Your corps may have a discipling group for new converts. That's an excellent start. If your corps has soldiership preparation classes in which discipling also takes place, that's also helpful. Does your corps do lifelong discipling? If not, consider ways discipling can be incorporated into everything that takes place in the corps. This continuity of discipling is so important because discipleship is a lifelong journey of intimacy with Jesus, learning more, loving better, and serving more helpfully. In this journey we face new challenges every day and are often called upon by Jesus to take a turn into a new situation for which we may not feel prepared. Your corps can (and should) be a place where we get the help we need for this journey.

Attention must also be given to the ways we are discipled. Remember, as the journey of a disciple of Jesus is a lifelong affair; so it is also a lifelong learning. We never "arrive" as a disciple, never reach the place where further growth in grace, further development of our gifts and abilities, and further honing of our skills as disciples are not needed. We cannot learn to be a disciple in one fell swoop or in a ten-week discipling course—although the course would be a good place to start! We cannot learn it solely through the Sunday sermon—although preaching that focuses on how to live the life to which Jesus calls us is very helpful. We must learn it primarily step by step. Discipleship is a day-by-day lifelong journey.

Consider the apostle Peter, a passionate, impulsive disciple if there ever was one. As you encounter him again and again in the Gospels, you sometimes see him as someone who gets something very right (**Matthew 16:13-17**), only to turn around and get the next thing very wrong (**vv. 21-23**). He is the one whose faith in Jesus is so strong he accepts Jesus' invitation for him to walk on water to get to Him (**Matthew 14:28-28**), only to begin sinking when in the next moment he becomes distracted by a rising wind (**vv. 30-32**). At the end of those intense three years of being discipled by the teaching and life modeling of Jesus, his courage as a disciple fails him when, for his personal safety, he denies that he even knows Jesus (**Mark 14:66-72; Matthew 26:69-75; Luke 22:56-62; John 18:16-18, 25-27**), a cowardice for which later the resurrected Jesus calls him to account without having to say a word. Peter fully understands his failure at this testing and receives the forgiveness he sees in Jesus' eyes (**John 21:15-19**). And we learn that after Peter has become an apostle for Christ, it takes a crazy vision in a dream of a huge sheet full of un-kosher animals, with a voice that says, "Take and eat," to get him to understand and then act on a gospel that includes *everyone* in its scope (**Acts 10**). Years later the lesson still hasn't fully sunk in because he refuses to eat with Gentile Christians in Antioch and has to be disciplined by Paul (**Galatians 2:11-14**).

Considering all this, it is astounding that Jesus never gives up on His intention that Peter play a key role as shepherd of Jesus' flock (the church), in fact that he be the kind of rock on which the Christian church is to be built! Over-confident, legalistic Peter—a chosen shepherd for Jesus? Wavering, error-prone Peter—a steady rock for the church? How crazy is this?

It's actually good news for us all. Very good news. It's good news, first, because it demonstrates that Jesus doesn't give up on His disciples. With all of Peter's failings, He doesn't abandon him. With all of our misunderstandings, mistakes, and missteps, Jesus works patiently with us as He leads us into the next phase of our disciple journey with Him. The other part of the good news is that the profile of Peter's growth as a disciple of Jesus is not that different from ours. Our development as disciples is also step-by-step, most of them small, a few of them more dramatic, others not so dramatic but profoundly life-altering.

The journey, however, is not a straight line forward. There are regressions. One regression is when we grow lax in some aspects of discipleship because we haven't been paying attention, or giving attention to how Jesus is calling us to move forward to a new stage of the journey. We regress spiritually in that situation because if a living organism isn't growing, it is dying. The other kind of regression is more serious. It is when we become both complacent and compromised. We may be swayed to return to old ways, or we may reach a level of fear about what the next phase of our disciple journey will ask of us. We backslide, as Peter did after Jesus' arrest. The good news is that Jesus doesn't abandon us. He waits for us as His Holy Spirit gently urges us to return to the journey.

Important to this restoration are our fellow Christians, our church, in our case the corps family. In fact, our fellow Salvationists are essential for the whole journey. Our journey with Jesus, our growth as disciples, does not take place in a vacuum. We travel with Jesus in the company of our spiritual family. This fellowship is not a coincidence, it's a necessity.

It isn't a convenience, it's an absolute need. As the apostle Paul put it, our congregation (corps) is the Body of Christ, every member of which needs the others. We support and build up each other on an ongoing basis. We are a spiritual family (**Romans 12:3-17; I Corinthians 12:12-27**).As the Body of Christ, not only do we need each other, *we disciple each other.* We grow as disciples by praying for one another, by sharing our challenges, hopes, and fears, searching Scripture together, and holding each other accountable. This can happen in discipling groups, in twos, or under the spiritual direction of a wise and mature spiritual leader. It can happen at the corps, in a home, over lunch in a quiet restaurant, or in any place conducive to conversation and prayer. And it is most helpful if it takes place regularly.

I suspect one of the reasons many corps have soldiers and adherents that have not been discipled is that we move them straight from conversion to soldiers' preparation class where we talk briefly about our history, our purpose, our peculiarities and practices, our doctrines, and what is expected of soldiers, and then they're enrolled as soldiers. Some corps may incorporate discipleship training during this span, and that is a good step.

There is an even better step: Begin with the discipling immediately after conversion! By far the most important thing of all is that our converts become disciples of Jesus. Our Lord is not at all interested in people becoming Salvationists if they are not disciples or are not well on the way to becoming disciples. Nor does He want Methodists who are not disciples, Presbyterians who are not disciples, Catholics who are not disciples, etc. Membership is not discipleship. This would not be an issue if discipleship were not the whole point of Jesus' incarnation, life, death, and resurrection. He came to save us so that we can be His disciples. The discipleship is hard work. We don't become disciples simply because we're enrolled as soldiers or adherents. A true Salvationist is first of all a disciple.

Yes, the discipling can be a part of the soldiers' preparation classes. It should actually be the major part, and it should *continue* in some form after the preparation classes are over. Otherwise, the new soldier/adherent will conclude that further discipling is unnecessary, and nothing could be further from the truth of God's will. The Christ at our door always has a new invitation to extend to us to "grow in the grace and knowledge of our Lord and Savior Jesus Christ" (**II Peter 3:18**).

True imitators

Our Army has a future only if Salvationists are committed to live as imitating followers of Jesus. The Salvationist who claims, "I know [Christ]," while not keeping His commandments is not Jesus' disciple. "But the love of God is truly perfected in whoever keeps His word. This is how we know we are in Him. The one who claims to remain in Him ought to *live in the same way as He lived*" (**I John 2:4-6,** italics added). That's what a disciple is: someone who follows Jesus' example. Our corps are faith communities called to help us do precisely that.

There are other directions a corps congregation can take. There is a form of righteousness that complacent Salvationists who follow a tamed Jesus can live out. It is a parading righteousness, which may bring admiration, but ignores the secret sins of the heart. Jesus asks us to own up to the hidden sins, confess them, and seek reconciliation (**Matthew 5:21-24**). A compromised corps congregation lives only for itself, exercising the narrow holiness of its tamed Jesus by consciously or unconsciously excluding "those who don't fit their own profile." Their narrow righteousness ignores the primary focus of Jesus' mission as described in His mother Mary's prophetic *Magnificat:* Jesus embodies God's holiness by bending down to us in mercy and lifting up the humble and filling the hungry with good things (**Luke 1:52-53**). And as Matthew's Gospel presents it so poignantly in the words of Jesus, such self-emptying love and countercultural mercy is the mark of those who are His true disciples—and they live this way from the heart so naturally and self-effacingly, they can't even remember what their love has done (**Matthew 25:31-46**). You really know you're a disciple if, more and more, living like Jesus becomes natural. No wonder it's a lifelong journey!

The Christ at our door invites us to walk with Him and learn His way. We do it by studying and adopting His path and profile in Scripture, by finding and emulating Christ-like qualities in fellow Christians, and by risking Jesus' holy life and love daily as we live our lives in the world we inhabit.

FOR REFLECTION & PRAYER

What Scripture verse or passage in this chapter spoke most deeply to you, or challenged you most? Say why.

Barriers to discipleship

Personal: Identify one thing in your own life over which you have personal control that you suspect is an impediment to your discipleship. What step(s) could you take to break that barrier to free yourself to follow Jesus better?

Your corps: Identify one thing in your corps that you suspect may stand in the way of helping Salvationists develop as disciples. How could you helpfully share your concern with the corps officer and other members?

Every Salvationist a disciple

Personal: Having identified and broken the personal barrier described above, what specifically could you do now in order better to model your own life after Jesus?

Your corps: Following your conversation with your corps officer or a group in the corps over a barrier to members developing as disciples, what do you think our Lord would then want to take place in the corps?

True imitators

Personal: What aspect of the life that Jesus modeled for us would you like to improve in your own life? What step could you take to do this?

Your corps: Describe (a profile of) your corps as a community of disciples seeking to imitate Jesus. Suggest something specific the corps could do to be more intentional about it (avoid generalities and vague wishes!).

CHAPTER 4

BE WILLING TO CHANGE

If we are to better the future we must disturb the present.
(Catherine Booth)

A Church which pitches its tents without looking out con-
stantly for new horizons, which does not continually strike
camp, is being untrue to its calling. The historical nature of
the Church is revealed by the fact that it remains the pilgrim
people of God. (Hans Kung, *The Church*)

In Chapter One we looked at the first key to our future:
what it means for us actually to believe that Jesus is Lord.
We said that "Jesus is Lord" is far more than a creed; it is a
way of being we call holiness. Chapter Two sought to define
a true Biblical holiness as an intimate relationship, a total way
of life, and a calling to go into the world. In Chapter Three
we saw that holiness is also a radical way of living called
discipleship. In this chapter we're going to look at *changes.*
The Christ at our door calls us to a lifetime of change. How
willing are we? How willing are we to *be* changed, and how
willing to *cause* change?

Some of you may be saying to yourselves, "Do we *have* to
talk about change? I'm tired of change!" I share those reser-
vations. Change is happening so fast in the world around us
it makes us dizzy. Our world is an ever-blowing whirlwind of
change. Many have even said that change is the only thing

we can rely on any more. We can rely upon the ground shifting, fashions altering, values changing, people moving—all at a faster and faster pace. We revisit a place of fond memories and find it to be very different, and not a necessarily better place. Yesterday's adequacies become today's inadequacies. Yesterday's truth becomes today's irrelevance. Today's latest gadgets—car, computer, whatever—quickly become so yesterday. Change, change, change. And where does it get us? Many studies confirm that our frantic consumerist behavior to keep up with the latest thing only provides very short-lived satisfaction, followed by dissatisfaction and a resumption of the drive for better still. And it never ends, until the end.

Most of our addiction to change is based on bigger-and-better-for-me-and-mine. And if that isn't what motivates you, well, you don't fit into the prevailing culture very well. In the face of it all, some Christians, it seems, have decided to retreat from the world and huddle down behind their religious barriers while they wait for the Lord's return. It's true that many (if not most churches) have become bastions against change, a place to go to get out of the incessant pressure to adapt to the ever shifting landscape. A place where nothing changes, and neither do the church members. Other Christians, it seems, have adopted a certain kind of blessings theology: God loves you and He *wants* you to have all the up-to-date things. They're not changing either: they can be relied on to keep running after the latest and biggest and, if need be, to accommodate Christian values along the way.

The change we are talking about in this chapter is something very different. We're not talking about adapting or not adapting to rapid social change. We're talking about the changes *God* wants to make in our lives and in the world around us. The apostle Paul speaks of "a good work" that God begins in us, finally completed "by the day of Christ Jesus" (**Philippians 1:6**). He says that he is still in pursuit of God's goal for his life, "God's upward call in Christ Jesus," and that "all of us who are spiritually mature" will see their own lives in the same way, as a journey of personal change (**3:12-15**). "So let's press on to maturity," says the writer to the Hebrews, "by moving on from the basics about Christ's world... We're going to press on, if God allows it" (**Hebrews 6:1-3**). The Thessalonian church in particular is successfully making the changes of God's continuing good work in their lives. Their "faithfulness is growing by leaps and bounds," and "the love that all of [them] have for each other is increasing." Paul is so impressed by their progress that he's holding them up as a model for other churches (**II Thessalonians 1:3-5**). Followers of Jesus live in a world of continuing growth: their own. We all are the Holy Spirit's growth project.

As God's ever-growing, ever-changing disciples, He further expects us to be His change agents in the world. He has a plan "to bring all things together in Christ, the things in Heaven along with the things on earth" (**Ephesians 1:9-10**). We are a part of that plan, so we fully equip ourselves for the revolution (**6:10-17**). Our strategy is to "defeat evil with good," to overtake our enemies with compassion (**Romans 12:20-21**). As Jesus has reconciled the world to God through the Cross, we, the reconciled have been given the message and ministry of reconciliation (**II Corinthians 5:18-19**). Born of God, keeping the commandment of love, we defeat the world through faith in God's Son (**I John 5:3-5**). We are Christ's fellow workers in changing the world (**I Corinthians 3:9; Philippians 2:13**).

We are Jesus' Kingdom-of-God seed-sowers who reap a harvest beyond our understanding (**Mark 4:26-29**), sometimes revealed only later at harvest time (**Matthew 13:24-30**). The Kingdom of God is here to stay, and we are called to expose it, live it, and turn it loose on the world.

We're not talking about a belief in our capacity to make things happen—whatever "things" may mean. Nor is it confidence in the things themselves that we make happen. Sometimes we make changes that don't turn out well. It is, rather, to live in the confidence in a change that God made in the life and death of Jesus, described by Jesus as an accomplished fact in **John 12:31** and **16:33**: He has *already* overcome the world! The question for us is: How do we live in the confidence of that victory? How do we live in the world not so much as a challenge we must meet but as a victory we must find out how to live with and by? The victory is there, often hidden, and we are called to trust it and pay the price for that trust. Such trust will change us and enable us to be Christ's change agents in the world.

Think of our Lord as a young Jesus, submitting to John's baptism, the marking and public announcement of a changed direction in His life. Then testing the change in a forty-day fast, with Satan unleashing his most penetrating arrows to kill the calling and undermine the possibility that sinners can be changed into saints. And Jesus emerges from the trial, says Matthew's Gospel, with a *new message*: "Change your hearts and lives! Here comes the Kingdom of heaven!" (**Matthew 4:17**). We, His disciples, are all about that change. That change is the pathway for our calling.

On the authority and with the guidance of Scripture, I believe that all Christians—and this means all Salvationists, as well—are called to bring change in three areas. First, Jesus calls us to change *ourselves*. Second, He calls us to change *our corps*. And then, He calls us to change *the world*. These callings are what we'll explore in the remainder of this chapter.

Jesus calls us to change OURSELVES

One of the ways we distort our Wesleyan heritage is to think that when we have experienced entire sanctification we have arrived. All our motives are now pure, perfect love is now unquestionably the source of all our actions, and all we have to worry about is protecting and not losing the blessing. As if all of life is now straight-lined. (That view makes me wonder why saintly Lt. Colonel Lyell Rader felt he had to be the first one to the altar when the appeal was given in the Holiness Meeting.)

The truth is, the sanctifying work of the Holy Spirit is what puts us in the place spiritually where we're now *ready* to start making the most significant changes, and to do it for the rest of our lives. Life is growth, spiritual life is growth in grace. At the very beginning of Peter's Second Letter, the apostle prays that church congregations "may...have more and more grace and peace through the knowledge of God and Jesus our Lord" (**II Peter 1:2**). More and more. And at the very end of the letter he instructs them to "grow in the grace and knowledge of our Lord and Savior Jesus Christ" (**3:18**). Grow, grow, grow.

I recently came across John Wesley's response to a letter

from a Mrs. Pawson in which the lady evidently argued for a life of continued growth in holiness: "You do well to strongly insist," he wrote, "that those who do already enjoy (sanctification) cannot possibly stand still. Unless they continue to watch and pray and aspire after higher degrees of holiness, I cannot conceive not only how they can go forward but also how they can keep what they have already received" (*Letters*, VIII, 184, quoted in Winekoop, 57).

In **Ephesians 4:11-16** the apostle Paul talks about the leadership gifts God gives to the church: apostles, prophets, evangelists, pastors, and teachers. For what purpose? That we, in unity with one another and in the knowledge of God's Son, move beyond our spiritual infancy and grow toward the whole measure of the fullness of Christ. And then he tells us what the outcome of the growth journey is: We are able to use our various ministry gifts to "build ourselves up in love." More and more we favor our compassionate Christ, like healthy branches of the life-giving vine (**John 15:5**).

There is a reason why Jesus used organic metaphors—crops growing slowly but surely, a tiny mustard seed miraculously transformed into a huge plant, flowers of the field unfolding their startling beauty causing us to catch our breath. He is describing how the Kingdom of God sneaks in quietly and then startles us with its presence and power. Metaphors of organic growth. There is a reason Paul, in **Romans 12** and **I Corinthians 12**, compares the church to a human body, a living thing that either grows, or it declines and dies. The same truth applies to our spiritual lives. We grow, or we backslide and eventually die spiritually. Why would we not, rather, choose to live a life of becoming more and more like Jesus?

Well, what does this mean? I think Wesley was right when he identified the love of God and the compassion of Christ as the key markers. Jesus said it in the words I previously suggested could be the Christian's *Shema*: ". . . love the Lord your God with all your heart, with all your being [soul], with all your strength, and with all your mind, and love your neighbor as yourself" (**Luke 10:27**). Grow in loving God, and everyone.

It's that "everyone"—that's the stumbling block, isn't it? It's the person in the corps congregation you most can't abide. God says, I send them to you to keep you in grace, because you can't love *that* person without grace. That person is God's special gift to you and me. Same with the obnoxious next-door neighbor. Jesus doesn't even allow us to hate terrorists. "Love your enemies"—all of them. Talk about a lifetime of growth challenges!

Perhaps we also grow most when we, at personal cost, make sacrifices for the benefit of some person or group of people we don't even know. David Guy reminds us of a decision of 6,000 nineteenth-century mill workers in Manchester, England. It was a time, says Guy, when "Christian faith was robust in the English working classes." These workers made the decision to write a letter to Abraham Lincoln "urging him to continue the fight for the abolition of slavery even though the Civil War had resulted in their own unemployment because no cotton was reaching the mills where they were employed." Lincoln was deeply moved, and in reply to their letter he called their self-sacrificing act "sublime Christian heroism" (*Salvationist*, 9/19/98, p. 7). Yes, says Jesus, go ahead and don't stand up for what *you* deserve; instead stand up for justice and mercy for someone else. Startle others with your holy humanity. "Love your neighbor," says Jesus, and *especially* those who are worse off than you.

And just when you think you've mastered that command, Jesus brings along...Who? The next challenge to our loving. Parker Palmer says the community you live in—maybe your neighborhood, maybe your church (corps)—is the place the person you least want to live with lives.

Jesus doesn't ask us to change just at the beginning of our journey with Him. He asks us time after time to make a change to allow His love even more gracefully to flow through us, like an unexpected blessing on someone's life. And so we keep changing, keep growing, so we can be more like Jesus and less like what people normally expect of someone. Yes, Christ stands at the door that is our lives, forever calling us to let Him change us toward His likeness.

Jesus calls us to change OUR CORPS

We easily forget that Jesus focused His mission on those who didn't fit the desirable public profile. Those who did—the religious leaders, the powerful, the wealthy—had to seek Him out (**John 3:1; Mark 10:17-22**), invite Him to dinner (**Luke 11:37**), or arrest Him to get an audience (**Matthew 26:57; Mark 15:1**). And the apostle Paul *really* opened the floodgates with his obsession with letting the Gentiles—*i.e.*, everyone else!—into Jesus' family. And centuries later the likes of the Wesleys, the Booths, and then the Pentecostals went in the same expansive direction. All of them calling us to open up and welcome in, as well as reach out and go out to the others of our world.

You think maybe we need to be reminded? We Salvationists have come a long way from our beginnings with the marginalized, a long way from our own roots. We have a marvelous array of social services that are largely for the marginalized (something for which, by the way, I am proud). Of course, we shouldn't force Jesus on those we serve, who are, by virtue of needing our services, in the weaker position. Coming to Jesus through hypocritical compliance to our invitation (or subtle pressure) in order to obtain the most service from us demeans both the recipient and the helper, not to mention compromises the integrity of the Gospel and the freedom of the person. Nevertheless, while avoiding such manipulation of the people we serve for statistical conversions, should we not ask ourselves the question: What percentage of those we help in these services become followers of Jesus Christ because of the Christly compassion they experience with us and our openness to respond to their spiritual search? What percentage of Christians we help are also helped on their spiritual journey? How close do we get to them, how much of their lives do they share? How much of the holy love of Jesus do we give ourselves opportunity to share with them? Are we in mission with them in a deeper way, or just dispensing temporary help? Maybe your corps can respond positively to these questions, but I don't think most corps and service centers in the Western world can. Otherwise the number of Salvationists probably wouldn't be declining so steadily in North America, Europe, Australia, and New Zealand. The simple cup of cold water (or any temporary help) in Christ's name is an act of beauty in itself. Failure to respond where there is spiritual openness, however, is a missed opportunity to engage at the real center of a person's life.

And what about your own corps congregation? Unless a corps has a vibrant rubber-meets-the-road kind of outreach in its community, and unless it has a let's-get-out-there-and-be-Jesus-in-the-world kind of mindset, it is not the corps God has called it to be. Salvationists without hospitality to strangers and the courage of foreign-turf invaders are not really true Salvationists.

One of the mistakes made by some of the early church growth proponents was to make a sharp distinction between those who have gifts for mission and those with maintenance gifts. All of God's people, all followers of Jesus, are in fact called to mission. Just because a gift seems on the surface to be best utilized within the corps, we should not exclude it from missional service. For example, Salvationists with the gift of hospitality are shortsighted if they think this means the exercise of their gift is confined to welcoming worshipers or preparing or serving corps dinners. The gift becomes missional, however, when private homes become places of hospitality to neighbors. The house churches of the early Christian movement were legendary places and platforms for mission.

The gift of administration, which seems at first to be designed only for some oversight role, financial responsibility, or stewardship planning in the corps, can also be employed in one's neighborhood or work to help people manage their life and/or resources. The gift of pastoral care can be used to help shepherd people in the corps through challenging life situations, but also similarly to help people in one's neighborhood or work. *Whatever* gifts a Salvationist has, they can and should be used missionally. In the offering of oneself to another in this way, a trusting relationship will usually develop and sometimes this further (and happily) leads to a person coming to faith in Jesus.

There are, indeed, spiritual gifts that are mission-specific. Evangelism is one example; social services another. These are gifts and skills essential to a corps' mission. But does this mean that a Salvationist that doesn't have the *gift* of evangelism is not called to be an evangelizer, to give inviting testimony to the non-believer by his life and his witness? Indeed, the world will not discover Jesus unless the whole nation of Christians lives the life of Jesus in the world **(Matthew 5:13-16)** and speaks of Jesus either frequently **(Acts 4:20)** or more strategically **(Proverbs 25:11; I Peter 3:1-2)**, as the Spirit leads. Nor will the world discover Jesus unless the whole nation of Christians serves others helpfully, modeling themselves after Jesus' own servanthood **(Luke 22:27; John 13:14-15; Matthew 25:40)**, serving even beyond their comfort level.

If we're going to let God change this Army we love, we're going to have to let Him mobilize us and get us praying for, welcoming in, connecting with, reaching out and going out to this world He wants us to love back into His family. I think He'd like a lot more help from us.

This all has everything to do with our journey in holiness. The truly holy people are up to their necks in the world. Why? Because holiness has everything to do with the world. What earthly good—or Heavenly good, for that matter—is a private holiness?! What good is it to the mission for which God called this Army into being? Holiness is not real unless it is embodied, unless it is lived out with courage in the world, unless it takes on the flesh and blood of up-front, personal engagement with people—and especially those living on the margins. This is rubber-meets-the-road holiness; this is radical discipleship. This is what people do who really believe Jesus is Lord over all, and for all. **(Matthew 5:13-16; 25:40; Philippians 2:12-18; Titus 2:11-12)**

Every one of our corps and all Salvationists are called to engage the world in this way, whether through a detention center for teenagers, or a nursing home with some residents who have been abandoned by their families, or the elderly couple up the street who live in a hell of loneliness, or the families of a nearby, impoverished community who can't make it on their minimum wage and are getting further behind each month, or even a fellow service or social club member shattered by a bitter divorce or an embarrassing business failure. What catches your eye; what moves your heart? The Christ at your door may be calling you to make a difference there in His name. A holy mission is waiting for every one of us, and if only half of us respond, it will change our corps—so much so that the other half will probably get on board eventually, and those who don't will only, and sadly, stew in their chosen path of passivity, or go somewhere else where they won't have to hear Jesus and obey Him.

We've already come to the third thing we must be willing to change: the world.

Jesus calls us to change THE WORLD

During the time when the change in name from The Christian Mission to The Salvation Army was being finalized, William Booth announced: "The Christian Mission...has organized a salvation army to carry the blood of Christ and the fire of the Holy Spirit into every corner of the world" (*The Christian Mission Magazine,* Sept. 1878). From that time on, international expansion of the mission took place at breathtaking speed. The Salvation Army became a world mission!

The target of God's mission is the world. "God so loved the world" (**John 3:16**). The text does not say the church, or The Salvation Army. It says *the world.* It was for the world that Jesus lived and died. We are all called to participate in this all-the-world mission, this mission of God. In the days of the Wesleys, pastors and priests tended to say, "The parish is my world." John Wesley said, "The world is my parish." By the time the Booths came along, many Methodist churches had abandoned their founder's world vision, and their ministers tended to focus on their congregations. What, then, was the battle call of this young Salvation Army? "All the world!" And that name was given to the Army's world mission magazine, which exists to this day. This Salvation Army, said Booth, is "one vast missionary enterprise."

Yes, indeed, we want corps officers and local corps leaders to nurture spiritually strong corps congregations. We want a pastoral ministry of caring, and some fall too short in these areas. But the job isn't even half done if we are not cultivating a heart for the world and training Salvationists to look around them and start looking and acting like Jesus around people where they live their lives (**Mark 10:43-45; John 13:13-15,34-35; Romans 13:14; II Corinthians 4:10; Ephesians 5:1-2; Philippians 2:5-8; Colossians 3:10-11; I Peter 2:21; I John 2:6; 3:16; 4:17**). This is what true Salvationists do—true Christians, for that matter. In fact, it's how real holiness expresses itself.

From the very beginning of His three-year mission, Jesus made it clear that His mission was not primarily for those who were privileged economically and socially (**Luke 4:14-21**). And then later on, don't you know it, Luke records that Jesus checked out of Galilee and launched a ministry in Samaria, described from **Luke 9:51** all the way to **19:18**! It was bad enough that Jesus had concentrated His mission in Galilee. (When Philip had told Nathanael that Jesus was from a town in Galilee called Nazareth, Nathanael, though originally from Galilee himself, had asked, "Can anything from Nazareth be good?" [**John 1:46**] The town itself was quite small and politically insignificant.) Purist Judean Jews didn't exactly see Galilee as a model Jewish province. But Samaria was even worse. It was the neighboring province most despised by Judean Jews! Its residents were seen as mongrel Jews at best. For heaven's sake, what's going on with this indiscriminate mission of Jesus?

The whole world was Jesus' parish from the beginning, though at the time it extended no further than Palestine. "Thy Kingdom come," He taught us to pray, "Thy will be done, on *earth* as it is in Heaven." "Well, good luck, Jesus. We wish you every success, because this world seems pretty hopeless to us. But if anyone can do it, Lord, you can. We'll make it a matter of daily prayer." "Oh," says Jesus, "I really can't, because I'm not that kind of Son of God. I've chosen *you* to get out there in the world and prepare the way for Me. I didn't make a mistake when I chose you for this, and I'm going to stick by My decision. You are My disciples, which means I'm your teacher and model. Your job is to imitate Me. So, get on out there and do your job."

It's worth mentioning that there are two ways John Wesley's theology helps us here. First of all, he believed in what Wesleyan scholar Timothy Tennent calls "mobile holiness," a holiness that is lived, and should be lived, *anywhere and everywhere.* As the song says, "We are witnesses for Jesus [even] in the haunts of sin and shame." "Mobile holiness," says Tennent, "is viral, and there is no part of creation which it does not declare to be under the Lordship of Jesus Christ! We claim the 'whole field'—no privatized religion for us!" (Timothy Tennent, "Four Wesleyan Doctrines," internet). Mobile holiness.

Second of all, we should be eternally grateful for the strong (and correct) emphasis Wesley placed on the doctrine of *prevenient grace*, the grace that goes before us. Paul says in **Ephesians 1:22-23** that "God placed all things under [Jesus'] feet, and appointed Him to be head over everything for the church, which is His body, the fullness of Him who fills everything in every way." Wherever we find ourselves, Jesus is already there, claiming His territory. The risen Christ does away with all the separations that make us uncomfortable, suspicious, afraid: Greek or Jew, circumcised or uncircumcised, barbarian, Scythian, slave, free. We can all update that list to apply to the different-nesses in people and cultures that threaten us and limit our mission. And then we can say with Paul: God is "over all, through all, and in all"! (**Ephesians 4:6**). No one can keep out God's prevenient grace! Jesus is everywhere we live our lives, waiting for us to join Him. Indeed, He's knocking at our door.

FOR REFLECTION & PRAYER

What Scripture verse or passage in this chapter spoke most deeply to you, or challenged you most? Say why.

Jesus calls us to change ourselves

Personal: Where in either your spiritual life or your ministry (service) do you feel you have become stagnant and desire further growth? What step(s) could you take to grow yourself in that area?

Your corps: What changes would you like to see in your corps that would encourage the spiritual growth of Salvationists, or break up a current complacency in the life of the corps? Who can you helpfully talk to about this?

Jesus calls us to change our corps

Personal: Name a specific challenge in your own life with respect to being more inclusive toward a group of a different ethnicity, generation, (or another wall of separation) that you are not entirely comfortable with. What specifically could you do to put yourself in a position to allow the Holy Spirit to open you toward that group?

Your corps: Is there a barrier in your corps to inclusiveness? If so, describe it. (The barrier may not be apparent on the surface, it may be hidden and still strong.) What could you do personally to help break it down?

Does your corps encourage Salvationists to use their spiritual gifts in mission when they're not at the corps? Is there a need for improvement? If so, what do you think could be done?

Jesus calls us to change the world

Personal: Honestly assess the seriousness of your own calling to be in mission when you are not at the corps (family, neighborhood, work, recreation, entertainment, etc.). What specifically could you do to strengthen your response to that calling?

Your corps: How well does your corps prepare you to follow Jesus (personally and publicly) when you are not at the corps? What specific step(s) could the corps take better to prepare you and other members for living out a worldly and mobile holiness?

PART TWO:

THE COMMUNITY
CHRIST INVITES US OUT
TO BE HIS CHURCH

At that time you were without Christ. You were aliens rather

than citizens of Israel, and strangers to the covenants of

God's promise. In this world you had no hope and no God.

But now, thanks to Christ Jesus, you who were once so far

away have been brought near by the blood of Christ.

Christ is our peace. He made both Jews and Gentiles into

one group. With His body, He broke down the barrier of

hatred that divided us. He canceled the detailed rules of the

Law so that He could create one new person out of the two

groups, making peace. He reconciled them both as one body

to God by the cross, which ended the hostility to God.

— Ephesians 2:12-16

CHAPTER 5

GET OUR STORIES STRAIGHT

We need to become story-tellers again, and so mul-
tiply our ministry by calling around us the great
witnesses who in different ways offer guidance to
doubting hearts... One of the remarkable qualities
of the story is that it creates space. We can dwell
in a story, walk around, find our own space. The
story confronts but does not oppress; the story in-
spires but does not manipulate. The story invites us
to an encounter, a dialog, a mutual sharing ... As
long as we have stories to tell each other there is
hope. (Henri J.M. Nouwen, The Living Reminder)

Jesus didn't found a church. I mean that in the usual sense of the word and all that comes with it: a building, a paid minister (corps officer) who has been trained in seminary (training college), established doctrines, orders and regulations, a hierarchy that holds most of the church's (corps') power, a budget, standardized/approved policies—you get the idea. Read the four Gospels especially and even the rest of the New Testament, and you realize that that was not what He set up.

The Greek word we translate as "church" was probably not used by Jesus when He was teaching. It does appear three times in Matthew's Gospel and is spoken by Jesus Himself all three times, but not in the other three Gospels at all. (In **Mat-**

thew 16:18 Jesus says that on Peter the Rock he will build His church. In **Matthew 18:17** the word is used twice in reference to a dispute being brought before the whole body of believers.) Jesus, as best we know, didn't typically speak Greek because Aramaic was His native language, and even if He did speak Greek, for Him to speak Greek to the uneducated Palestinian crowds He taught would have been ridiculous. So, we don't really know the original Aramaic word He used to describe the particular community He was in the business of building. We simply have the Greek word that translated it.

But let's look at the Greek word itself. If we believe the Holy Spirit had a strong hand in guiding the New Testament writers to the proper Greek words to translate the Aramaic spoken by Jesus, then we can have confidence in that Greek word we translate as "church." The Greek word is *ekklesia*, which is comprised of two other Greek words: *ek* (out, out of) and *klesis* (a call, a calling). What is an *ekklesia*, a church? It is "the called out people of God." Yes, it is the faith community we're called *to*, but most importantly it is the community we are called out *from*. We go to it to be launched from it. And that's why the latter verses of all four Gospels, in one way or another, include a sending out (**Matthew 28:19-20; Mark 16:15; Luke 24:45-49; John 20:21**).

The word *ekklesia* is the word used for the followers of Jesus in Acts, the Letters, and Revelation. But it's never used in the sense that we usually use the word—as a building to go to, usually associated with and owned by one of a great number of Christian denominations. What we think of as a church is what the movement founded by Jesus evolved into over the centuries, as it became more and more a place to go to, and less and less a community to go out from.

So, how does a movement that began as a community of the "called out" evolve into a society of the "called in"? It happens something like this: Over time, as the movement expands, leaders get concerned about preserving the traditions of the movement, building an enduring structure, keeping a good reputation in the surrounding community, providing a system of rewards for those who work hardest and make significant contributions. The movement is systematized and regulated. And so, the movement evolves into an institution. There's nothing evil about that. It is going to happen if the movement is to survive.

But there is a danger. The danger is that the institution easily becomes absorbed with itself. Being "called to" becomes more important than being "called out." The institution often forgets the dominant reason for which it was called into existence: its mission, or maybe it simply spends less and less time on it. Perhaps the institution, sadly, comes finally to exist primarily for its own sake, and for the sake of those who run it. Maybe its overriding motivation becomes self-preservation. Over time it may even forget their Lord calling them to come outside and join His mission.

This has happened over and over again in the history of the Christian church. By the Fourth Century the church had become thoroughly institutionalized. Through the following centuries various movements occasionally sprang up to recall the church to the mission of its Founder, Jesus—for example, the Franciscan and Poor Clares Orders of laypersons who lived in poverty, imitated the life of Jesus, and brought the

Gospel to poor people. They were at first condemned by a church hierarchy embarrassed to have their own worldliness and negligence of the poor exposed. Then later, a thorn in the flesh of the church called Martin Luther came along, exposing the hierarchy's hypocrisy and exploitation. Then another thorn by the name of Wesley, embarrassing the church for its tolerance of spiritual laxity. Then the Booths, calling a privileged church to reach out and embrace the underprivileged.

There have been many other prophetic movements over the centuries since Christ, calling the church to be who and what *Jesus* called her to be. Over time they all seem to have institutionalized in some ways, and sadly it seems, for most of them the preservation of the institution and the power of those who ran it became more and more important, and the mission less so. Or maybe the mission became something different, maybe something easier and tamed, something done more decently and in order. Does a Christian movement always lose its mission when it becomes an institution? It can, but it doesn't have to. In this chapter we're going to invite you to remember the stories that shaped the early Christian movement, The Salvation Army, your own corps, your own personal life, and the lives of those Jesus is calling you to reach in our mission. Movements have stories, stories that shape them, inspire them, motivate them, define them. In the telling of stories, participants in the movement are reminded of who they are and what their mission is. Institutions have stories as well, but the stories tend to be overshadowed by doctrinal formulations and organizational rules and procedures, or relegated to what is considered to be a more elementary or primitive past, or reenacted in some sentimental way, or simply lost. Institutions have too many other things to think about and worry over. They are often in danger of living outside the story that shaped them and replacing it with another safer story, one that backs up what they have now become.

Where do we Salvationists first look to learn the stories that shape our lives? The answer is: the Bible.

The Bible's story

The Old Testament story begins with a God who creates everything and calls it good **(Genesis 1)**. The story focuses on His creation of humans, creatures reflecting the very image of God **(vv. 26-27)**. The humans (Adam and Eve) are given responsibility to multiply and also to care for and manage the earth **(vv. 28-31)**. Even better, they are endowed with the ability and privilege to commune with God. One gift, however, was challenging for humans and risky for God: the gift of freedom. God gave us ability to turn away from Him and pursue life on our own as if we were gods ourselves, knowing both the good and the evil. What this freedom entailed, therefore, was the option to abandon the image in which we were created **(2:16-17)**. God could never love those He created in His image without giving them the freedom to love Him or not to love Him in return. In other words, God's love for us, as does all genuine love between persons, comes with the possibility of pain, the pain of love's rejection.

As we know, humans did choose to violate their true humanity and follow the lure of independence and self-sufficiency, a life lived outside fellowship with God, their Creator and Lord **(Genesis 3)**. The overall sweep of the Old Testament plays out this story from one era to the next, with individual stories within the larger story and characters who themselves come to embody, in one way or another, the separation. This sets the stage for what happens over the course of the story of the whole Old Testament, as time and again humans reject God's love and pursue their illusions about their self-centered selves. Later in the story, Abraham is given the promise that his Hebrew tribe will be specially chosen to demonstrate righteous living before the world and recall the nations to the blessing of true worship and fellowship with God (**Genesis 18:16-19**), but this doesn't go well. So later still, the Law is given through Moses to get and keep Israel, God's chosen, on track (**Exodus 20 and following chapters**). The Law, however, proves powerless to reshape the idolatrous heart. God finally sends prophets to announce judgment and recall the still sinful people to repent. Then a new strand appears in the latter part of the Old Testament story: God will send a Redeemer, a Suffering Servant, a Messianic Figure who will open up a new future (**Isaiah 43:14-19**), a Kingdom of peace and righteousness (**9:2-7**) with a highway called the Way of Holiness down which will travel a people overtaken by the joy of a new redemption (**35:8-10**). The Old Testament story ends without an ending to it all. The story is not finished; the promise not fulfilled. All eyes are on the future.

The New Testament begins with the proclamation that this future has now begun with the birth of a messianic Savior named Jesus. The Gospels of Matthew and Luke quote Old Testament prophets, applying their foretelling to this birth and proclaiming this Jesus as the fulfillment of what God had promised (**Matthew 1:23; Luke 3:4-5**). The story line continues, only we learn it is God Himself, now incarnate (in human flesh), who has come to save us. God has become this man

Jesus, and as it turns out, He spends most of His time with poor and marginalized people. Jesus knows His Old Testament. He knows **Psalm 113:7-8**, "God lifts up the poor from the dirt/and raises up the needy from the garbage pile,/to seat them with princes—/with the leaders of His own people!" And in His inaugural sermon at His hometown synagogue in Nazareth, He takes the words right out of Isaiah's mouth (**Isaiah 61:1-2; 58:6**) and writes them like a banner over His own life: "The Spirit of the Lord is upon Me,/because the Lord has anointed Me./He has sent Me to preach good news to the poor" (**Luke 4:18**). It is a sign and confirmation of Jesus as the true Messiah that "the poor have good news proclaimed to them" (**Matthew 11:5d**).

These people who are the primary focus of Jesus' mission have spent little of their time in religious activity, rarely attending their local synagogue. Jesus teaches anyone who will listen how to live in a new way. It's called the Kingdom of God, and He's Lord of this Kingdom. He sends out disciples to proclaim this Kingdom through preaching and healing. The religious establishment sees it as a dangerous conspiracy—which it is for them!—so they conspire with the Roman government to arrest Him and execute Him as a criminal. Then comes the big surprise: Jesus' defeat and death is His victory. Jesus' love-sacrifice releases enough redemptive power for the whole human race (**John 3:16**). And then: the resurrection—God's love wins! (**I Corinthians 15:20-28**). The rest of the New Testament plays this story out by speaking it and living it throughout the Mediterranean world (**Acts 1:6-8**). And the New Testament concludes with the anticipation of the return of the resurrected Jesus, bringing together all nations and ethnicities, the first being last and the last first, into His now-fully-established Kingdom (**Luke 13:29-30**). The final words come from the mouth of the resurrected Jesus: "Yes, I'm coming soon." And the waiting church cries in prayer, "Amen. Come, Lord Jesus!" (**Revelation 22:20**).

The story is still not finished. It is left to us to get it straight, for it is not a tale to be told either as an entertaining drama or a formulaic prescription. It is a living story, inviting the whole human race to enter it and find themselves in it, with all their trials and troubles, blemishes and blotches, hopes and fears; to find themselves there as the recipients of God's unimaginable mercy and transformative love. Christ wants us fully to immerse ourselves and find ourselves in this story—to live in and for this story, to *be* this story for the world. For every Christian, including every Salvationist, this story is the foundation on which their life is built.

The Salvation Army's story

The early Salvation Army embraced this Bible story both in their living and in the focus of their mission. Following the example of Jesus, Salvationists invaded the places where they found the poorest and most marginalized populations: primarily in the cities and larger towns. Like an Old Testament army of prophets, they attacked the legions of hell that abused and degraded the industrial poor. Like New Testament witnesses they proclaimed a liberating Gospel. Their battlefield was a world of oppression, the world of urban poor who knew little or nothing of a saving Gospel, and certainly couldn't see it in the actions of churches so often aligned with the industries that exploited them and kept them in abject poverty. In the name of Jesus, bands of Salvationists paid the price of taking on all this oppression, believing they could save those considered unsave-able and beyond hope. If you want to see our movement's story in one picture, it's right there inside the early editions of William Booth's *Darkest England and the Way Out*: a vast sea filled with drowning men, women, and children (the exploited and demoralized) with an army of rescuers working in every way they can to rescue them and lead them to a better future in Christ.

It all began in the notorious East End of London. Here among the poorest, William Booth came to the conclusion he had found his destiny, as he reputedly announced to his wife Catherine one day. His son Bramwell remembers his father later taking him into an East End pub (bar) crawling with disheveled, depressed humanity and whispering to him, "These are our people. These are the people I want you to live for and bring to Christ" (Collier, p. 44). One Anglican bishop had described the churches' failure to reach the urban poor as "the one great church question of our time." Another clergyman came to the conclusion that the churches had not attracted the poor and working-class people because it offered no real place for them within its life. The Reverend J.F. Kitto went so far as to say that "amongst the working classes there is a feeling that they compromise themselves in some way by going to a church" (Inglis, *Churches and Working Classes in Victorian England*, p. 57).

The time was ripe for a Christian movement to bring the Gospel back to the world of the common people, whence it had come in the first place. It was time for disciples of Jesus to humble themselves and follow the downward movement of their Lord's Incarnation (**Philippians 2:7**) with reckless abandon. This was precisely the mindset the apostle Paul said disciples must adopt and live out **(2:5)**. If the Gospel was not for the common people and the poor, it was for no one. If we do not go first to those to whom Jesus went, we are not really His disciples. The early Salvationists left the high altar gathering and relocated in the streets and hovels of the teeming slums. "These are our people," said Booth.

George Scott Railton lived this incarnational creed to the extreme. He passionately believed in getting as close to the common folk as possible. A Salvationist pioneer leader who traveled the globe on behalf of the General, he preferred the humblest accommodations and the cheapest means of transportation. As a disciple of the God who "emptied Himself," how could he accept any status himself? As a follower of the Lord who had nowhere to lay His head, how could he tolerate any luxury? On a voyage on a ship to Hong Kong and Korea, he had to pull a Chinese shirt over his Salvation Army tunic in order to be allowed to travel third class. After picking up bugs in the crammed quarters and enduring the endless cries of a host of babies, he wrote, "All that is only an appeal to any true Salvationist who cannot but wish to see and know life among the poorest" (Bernard Watson, *Soldier Saint*, p.219).

Perhaps the biggest scandal of early Salvationism lay in its determination not only to get right next to the commonest people, but also to speak their language, adopt their ways of self-expression, and practically start from scratch in developing a Christian community environment in which they felt at home. The end result was usually not dignified, but neither was the Bethlehem stable nor the criminal's cross on Golgotha. If the established churches were scandalized, so be

it. If they chose not to follow Incarnation's downward movement, so be it. If the sight and sound and smell of Christ's
inviting, inclusive presence among "the least of these" was
too offensive to civilized sensibilities, so be it.

When Professor J. Stuart Blackie visited a Salvation Army
meeting to check out this maligned movement for himself,
he was profoundly moved by "the sight more sweetly human
and more spiritually impressive" of humble sinners kneeling
at the Mercy Seat for forgiveness. The next morning, he wrote
what the experience had confirmed:

> ... I would [rather] fling wild words about
> with them, than slip through life a smooth-lipped slave
> of reputable forms. Far better with too much
> of zeal to swell, and hot, aggressive love
> than sit in cleanly state and fear to touch
> the clouted sinner...
> (Sandall, *The History of The Salvation Army*, II, p. 145)

This is the story of our Army, the story Stuart Blackie saw
being lived out in our Salvationist forbears. It is a narrative
patterned on the Bible's story. It is a narrative we must keep
alive, or we become a very different, settled-in Army. We're
good at celebrating the story, but we must not treat it as a
tradition to glory in, as we sometime like to do in plays and
musicals and Salvation Army history books. It's a story to
emulate in our own day, or we will be a Salvation Army that
only lives in its past, while at the same time violating that
past in the present. A corps needs to ask itself: How can we
discover the streams the Lord is making in the wasteland of
our world today? How can we help the Lord make a way in

the desert? How can our Salvationist story be told and lived in the world in which we now find ourselves? How can we be faithful to both the Bible's story and our Salvation Army movement story? I believe that Christ does not want us to forget or forego our Salvationist story; He invites us to live in it and to live it out in the world in new ways.

Our corps' story

Consider you own corps. What is her story? She does have a story, whether she is one-year-old or 100. Did she begin as the outpost of another corps? Was she a corps from the beginning? What was the original purpose for which she was planted? What did DHQ have in mind? Or was DHQ even aware that some group was meeting and missioning, and then gave their official blessing only after they discovered this spontaneous expression of a community in mission? What did the first soldiers have in mind? How and why did the story that is your corps begin to be written?

Your corps history is important, not only because it may make interesting and even colorful recalling and increase your emotional attachment to the corps, but especially because it may reveal her connection to the Army's story and to the Bible's story. What is it about your corps' story that demonstrates what Jesus called His first disciples to be and do? What is it that embodies our early Army at its missional best? Was there a time in her history when the evangelical passion waned? If so, was it ever recovered, and if so, how? If your corps is fairly new, has it begun yet to write a story worth telling, and if not, what is needed to get the story underway?

These are a lot of questions, but they are crucial for your corps. Some corps start well, and then over time go bad, or they become settled and stale. It's helpful to understand what happened and why, so that we are then in a position for God to help us get back and keep on track with a story worth telling. A corps may be living out a story of divisiveness, and her members need to learn how to allow the Holy Spirit to lead them back to unity in Christ. A corps may be succeeding by certain organizational measurements, but in times of honesty members suspect that there is a spiritual shallowness behind the corps' apparent success.

We understand the Bible only if we see it as one large overarching story, not as a collection of religious insights. We understand The Salvation Army only as we understand the big story that brought it into being as a missional force for God, a story that gives it purpose and strength so long as Salvationists live by it and are unified around it. The same goes for your corps. Draw and learn from her best days. If she has not had many good days over the years, and still doesn't, then, if you have the God-inspired will, conspire together to upset the rotten applecart and replace the contents with the fruit of the Spirit. Start over by learning the Bible's and the Army's real story of limitless mercy, saving grace, and sanctifying power. Today Christ is inviting your corps to embody the mission to which He has called our Army.

Personal stories

The Bible is comprised of many stories that together make up the one overarching story of redemption. Many of those stories are personal. In Scripture, we are told the stories of

Abraham and Sarah, Moses, Saul, David, Mary the mother of Jesus, Mary Magdalene, Mary and Martha, John the Baptist, Peter, Paul, John, and many others. Their stories play a key role in the story of God's chosen people in the Old Testament and in the movement that Jesus inaugurated. These people were not perfect, but they all teach us something important. The same is true of the story of The Salvation Army. It teems with key characters like William and Catherine Booth, George Scott Railton, Bramwell and Florence Booth, Samuel Logan Brengle, Evangeline Booth, Harry Williams, to name only a few. Again, they were not perfect, but their stories are key parts of fabric that is the Army's story. You will undoubtedly have other names that come to mind, Salvationists that may be a legend in your own territory or division, or who were key spiritual exemplars and influencers in the story of your own corps, even though they may have stayed out of the public spotlight. Whether you realize it or not, your own personal story is definitely a part of the larger story of your corps and by extension of the whole Army today.

What best defines and describes our Army and your corps are the personal stories that comprise them. Yes, our doctrines are important, but more important are the stories of God and His saving actions on behalf of the human race in particular and the whole universe in general. Our doctrines, in fact, are but intellectual distillations of those stories. Without the story of salvation there would be no Christian doctrines of real substance. Nor is our Army or our corps best defined and described by our system of government, our methods of organization, our orders and regulations, our programs, or our professional competencies. Behind all of this is the truly important thing: the people who are living stories of God at work. If we lose the stories, we lose our Army.

Who are these people? They are you, and they are all your fellow Salvationists. A corps is a community of Salvationists with stories. We honored these stories in our early days when public testimonies were a part of every public meeting. Stories are meant to be shared. Stories untold rob others of the help your story can give them. Some of our stories are filled with joy, and in the sharing we allow others the privilege of rejoicing with us. Some of our stories are about obstacles overcome, and in the sharing we encourage others to overcome their own obstacles. Some of our stories are filled with pain, even suffering, and in the sharing of the burden we trust the compassionate love of our brothers and sisters, and we allow ourselves to be comforted. (I say this with the full recognition that some suffering is so deeply painful and damaging [and possibly has been repressed for so long] it is best shared, at least at first, with a trusted counselor, or even a therapist. Nevertheless, those of your fellow Salvationists who are spiritually mature and personally perceptive will know that you are in pain and will lift you up in prayer.)

Whoever you are, your story is worth sharing. It will help you understand yourself better, and it will help others understand you. You may be surprised by your own story, by the way God has been at work in you over the years, regardless of the times you may have failed Him. You will undoubtedly be surprised by how many experiences shared by others are similar to your own. By sharing stories your corps will be drawn closer together. As stories are especially shared by people on a journey together, you and your fellow Salvationists will be encouraged to move forward in your journey with

Jesus because the Holy Spirit will teach you to keep the story going all your life. Your story never ends.

Christ calls us to share our own stories. Your story is important even beyond the boundaries of your corps congregation. Everyone you meet is a story. By sharing your story with others, you may well open the door to their stories. Your experiences will remind them of their own or of what they so deeply desire to find. You may be encouraging them on their own spiritual journey or motivating them to begin one. Your shared story will often be the best means you have of bringing someone to faith.

So it behooves us all to get our stories straight—the Bible's, the Army's, our corps', and our own. We are a people who have stories, share stories, and spread them wherever we are. We are God's storytellers. And God loves to tell His own story through us.

For Reflection & Prayer

Which Scripture verse or passage in this chapter spoke most deeply to you, or challenged you most? Say why.

The Bible's story

Personal: What is it in the story of either Israel or Jesus that most speaks to where you are in your own spiritual journey? What might your next important step be in your journey of faith?

Your corps: Where in the description of the Bible's story best describes where your corps is at the present time? Where would you like your corps to go next in its journey? Who could you talk to about this?

The Salvation Army's story

Personal: What part of the Army's story would you like to enter in a new way? What might that look like for you?

Your corps: What part of the Army's story would you like to see realized in your corps in a fresh and engaging way to serve our mission? Discuss this with someone or a corps group you think might also be interested.

Our corps' story

Personal: How much do you know about your corps' story (history)? If you don't know much, who could you best engage in conversation to learn as much as possible?

Your corps: In light of what you learn, describe where you think your corps is at the present time? Describe how you and others can help to move the story forward.

Our personal stories

Personal: What step do you sense the Holy Spirit is telling you to take in order to develop your own story as God is leading you? If you're not sure what that step is, what mature Christian could you reach out to for guidance?

Your corps: What could your corps do to encourage its members to be faithful to the Bible's story and live out the Army's story in its life and mission?

CHAPTER 6

DECIDE WHO WE ARE

Shall we be satisfied with going on as hitherto, picking up one here and one there, gathering together a more or less select congregation, forgetful meanwhile of the Master's command, "Go ye out into the highways and hedges, and compel them to come in?" The Salvation Army has taught us a higher lesson than this. Whatever may be its faults, it has at least recalled us to His lost ideal of the work of the church—universal compulsion of the souls of men.
(Bishop Dr. R.H. Lightfoot, Church of England)

I prefer a church which is bruised, hurting and dirty because it has been out on the streets, rather than a church which is unhealthy from being confined and from clinging to its own security.
(Pope Francis)

In the last chapter we talked about Jesus founding a movement rather than a church in the usual sense. We saw how important stories are to movements since movements are, in fact, discovering old and creating new stories of redemption and hope. Movements are stories in action. They are the heart of the true church, the moving-out people of God, which is actually the *true* meaning of church in the New Testament Greek word (*ecclesia*, the "called out" ones). People who are called out by God are under the spell of His world-saving story, and in the living out of His story they are writing new stories.

For many decades Salvationist leaders resisted calling their movement a "church" because the term reminded them of the exclusive sanctuaries and chapels that were anything but inviting to the poor and working-class populations of urban Great Britain. In fact, the Booths and other early leaders feared the possibility that the Army would become respectable and therefore an uncomfortable place for the impoverished. What "church" meant in those days carried far too much undesirable baggage for them. Only in recent decades have Salvationists (and not all of them) become comfortable with identifying the Army as a church. (In fact, this author was asked by IHQ to write a "Salvationist ecclesiology" in response to the World Council of Church's publication of an ecclesiology [a doctrine or theology of the church] for member churches. The WCC book title was *Baptism, Eucharist and Ministry.* The title of my book was *Community in Mission,* which had a stronger bias toward a movement mentality. It was published by IHQ in 1987, and republished with study guides by Frontier Press of the USA Western Territory in 2016. The book is not an official statement by The Salvation Army, only the views of the writer. The very fact of its publication by the international Salvation Army suggests, however, that there was much in the book that was consistent with Salvationist history, doctrine, and practice.)

It is now my view that our conversations around the matter of who we are as a Salvation Army and what our future is should take into consideration what we have learned generally about how and why movements begin, and how and why they become institutions—and specifically how and why

Christian movements (like the early church and the early Salvation Army) tend to follow this same evolution. The question we need to address is this: What is in danger of being lost in this transition, and how can the intention of the movement's founders continue to be realized, albeit in new ways? Or to put it differently, how can the movement mentality and mission continue to guide and shape the institution?

One indication of the institutionalizing of a movement is how members now relate to the movement story. We Salvationists may preserve the stories of the early days with pride—occasionally singing the early movement songs with great sentiment, fond remembrance, and blessing—all the while remaining in our corps enclaves. We may retain some of the exciting movement language and use it to label what we know deep down is no longer missionally effective. Or we may celebrate the inherited stories in readings, plays, or musicals performed in our corps, councils, and congresses, or watched on video, much to our inspiration and pleasure, but without real consequence in action. Another indication of institutionalizing is the actual changing of our stories themselves. As we become more concerned with ourselves, we talk more about how we have been blessed, or decry how we haven't. Or our stories relate more to what is or isn't happening within our corps. Inevitably, some of those stories relate to internal problems, interpersonal relationships, family fights, hurts and cruelties decades old but persisting beneath the surface to debilitate the present, and occasionally raising their heads in ugly confrontations. Some corps have actually forgotten all their original movement stories and are soldiering on in a vacuum of meaning, simply "playing Army" with no strong purpose or intention to win real missional battles.

When a movement's stories become sentimental celebrations or self-centered preoccupations, the movement has probably either betrayed or lost the reason for which it came into being. As a movement it is dying. It has failed to nurture its movement mentality and to discover a way forward to be God's missional people in this changing world into which we are called.

In this chapter, therefore, we will engage in the whole matter of deciding who we now are and who God wants us to be as a Salvation Army. What is the future into which God is leading us, and what does that future mean for the direction we must take today?

To answer these questions, it will be helpful first to place them in the larger context of the Christian movement as it evolved over the earlier centuries of its life.

Christianity: a movement that became an institution

[N]o institution escapes the ravages of time, however holy and great its founder.
(Carlo Carretto)

Christianity began as a movement and evolved into an institution. Church became a location where Christians gathered, a place to go to rather than be sent out from. (To this very day we may ask someone, "Do you go to church?" Or, "Where do you go to church?" We never ask, "What church sends you out?" Or, "Do you have a church that sends you out?") Because church became a set gathering place, worship became formalized and less personal. The priesthood (the religious professionals) became a heightened and the laity (the volunteers) a diminished position within the church. Priests (pastors) pre-empted ministry functions, robbing many lay people of their rightful callings. It was widely accepted that the institutional church was the only avenue to salvation and its rituals the only instruments for the forgiveness of sins and the granting of grace. The world outside the church was the place of sinning, and the church the place of repentance, absolution, and resolve—a kind of cleaners for dirty linen, with full knowledge the dirty linen would return the following week for another cleaning. Little was expected and done to help the laity live as holy and compassionate followers of Jesus Christ *in the world.*

It can and should be said, however, that over time movements arose in the church to recall Christians to the power of sanctifying grace, and as followers of Jesus to grow in grace and live holy lives in the world. Some of these movements continue to this day, either absorbed by the larger church, the sharp edges of their radical spirituality often blunted, or were sometimes tamed as they institutionalized themselves and became independent institutional church denominations.

Throughout the history of Christianity, a pattern developed: as a Christian movement evolves toward an institutional form, it becomes more concerned about its own internal issues and its survival in the world. Less and less is it concerned about its calling to evangelize and make disciples of nonbelievers, live out the radical ethics of Jesus in the world, and be a prophetic voice against exploitation and social injustice. More and more is it concerned about forming its own unique religious culture, instilling that culture in its members, and de-radicalizing its lifestyle in order for both the church and its members better to fit in to surrounding cultural norms and values. Extreme examples abound of compromises by established churches who actually strengthened oppressive governments, whether through cowardly silence or an addiction to the power brokers' blessing and support. Perhaps more common and less extreme, but equally damaging, the creeping intrusion and unconscious adoption of the values of the surrounding culture often compromised the prophetic integrity of the Gospel and of the church. The outcome of it all was a terrible and false conviction that persists to this day: People will not join or remain in the church if we don't water down the ethics of Jesus and expect less holiness. This is institutional thinking, the thinking of those who are so nervous about the church's survival they lower membership expectations and treat the saints only as exceptions to be admired rather than examples to encourage us all.

One type of Christian community that arises in reaction to the accommodations of the institutional church is the legalistic sect that supports a holy perfectionism in one form or another. Unlike a real Christian movement, it is primarily concerned about maintaining its holiness in *separation* from the world. It has clearly defined and very specific standards for holy living and is usually intolerant toward members who stray from this path. The community is happy for people to join them so long as they prove their holiness by complying with the standards. In these expressions of Christian community, judgment is strong and mercy is weak, and the wall between the community and the world is thick.

These forms of legalistic Christianity will usually attract

highly insecure people who choose to hide their need for grace behind the armor of their rigid religiosity. The holiness to which Jesus actually calls us is grace-based. It is an intimacy with Him that allows for our bumbling, and invites us to face our failings with His forgiveness. The intimacy encourages honesty about personal inadequacies and, in this environment of grace-filled acceptance, empowers us to grow further as holy disciples of Jesus. It is *this* spiritual landscape of a journey in grace, in and toward holiness, that characterizes the life of a Christian movement.

Is it possible for a Christian movement with a bias toward both holy living and compassionate mission to become over time a perfectionist sect with little or no missional commitment? Perhaps some expressions of our Army over the years have looked more like a sect than a missional movement. Our holiness has indeed on occasions become a perfectionism without grace. Our religious legalism has sometimes squelched our energy for mission. Instead of our holiness motivating mission as our Lord intends for it to do, it can be hardened into a forbidding righteousness like a hard, protective shell.

The Christian mission and movement is threatened by both a too institutionalized church and a too insulated sect. Christ, on the other hand, calls us to be a movement without either forbidding walls or a narrow, loveless holiness.

Keeping the Christian movement alive

We come, then, to the question that concerns us in this chapter. Can the institutional church and the perfectionist sect retain and cultivate a movement mentality and keep the movement alive? Can the movement continue to thrive within both the institutional church and the perfectionist sect? Some would say that once a Christian movement becomes an institution (a church, or a part of an existing church, or a sect), the focus and the way of thinking have already changed: the orientation is internal and the thought processes are usurped by questions of church programs, policies, and properties, or for the sect, spiritual perfection within the Christian community. The church or the sect is now about *us*, and while outsiders may be welcome to come to Sunday worship, for example, they are invited to join only if they're interested in becoming *like us*. Economic, cultural, ethnic, racial, and intellectual diversity is usually not highly valued. In other words, by their very nature institutional churches and sects tend to crush movement thinking and acting. Churches often think they have more than they can say grace over just keeping the ship afloat, without having to worry about what is happening in the lives of people outside its doors, which is what movements *are* particularly concerned about. Sects have plenty to worry about to keep members in line in accord with their strict definition of holy living.

Are these assumptions correct? Is God's predestined plan for Christianity that it first thrive as a movement, then organize as a church or a sect, followed by decline, then inevitable death? Is the Christian church like most other institutions of human history: they flourish, then decline, and eventually die? And then, perhaps, they start up again as a movement, only to repeat the cycle?

Perhaps some will argue that Christianity's movement phase was a more primitive or elementary beginning, necessary for the spread and eventual establishment of Christianity. Once this phase passes, the movement mentality has no more real use. Christianity has grown up; it has become an institution. The world will now be saved by our making *churches* so attractive, compelling, and sufficient for human needs that people will eventually flock to them and join the club. And why would people do that? Because our church has one or more of the best preachers, the best and most entertaining worship services, the most well-equipped community centers, family life centers that meet everyone's social, psychological, and educational needs, the most professional counseling centers, the best programs for fulfilling one's desire to serve his community, Bible studies second to none, personal growth groups, etc. Churches that have it all! The triumph of the institutional church!

The facts show otherwise. Some of the highly attractive churches seem to be thriving, but as Alan Hirsch shows in *The Forgotten Ways*, the very things that draw people to them will sooner or later be bested by an even more attractive church. These churches therefore tend to be recirculating Christians. Further, they often become empires, personal kingdoms of their now highly confident if not self-serving leader whose obvious motives now have no place in the Kingdom of God Jesus inaugurated. Other highly attractive churches are more traditional churches that desperately try to stop their declining attendance by coating their inward culture and outward stuffiness with such new things as a worship band, a digital screen, a lecture series on relevant topics (perhaps by an edgy speaker), or entertaining educational cruises. In spite of all these attempts to retain members and draw in new people, the memberships of traditional churches are still in decline.

(In the USA and in the entire Western World, The Salvation Army is also in decline.)

As for perfectionist sects, over time they will decline in numbers for lack of appeal to outsiders and from the suffocating atmosphere of their legalism and the killing effect of religion without mercy. The attraction to the insecure will prove to harbor a false hope. The law and its obsessions cannot save **(Mark 12:28-31; Matthew 22:34-40; Galatians 2:19-21; 3:10-12a; Romans 3:27-28; 7:1-6; 8:1-8).** The perfectionist sect is always on its way to extinction, save for the possibility of the Holy Spirit opening the heart of its members to grace over law and compassionate mission over holy seclusion.

The evolution of the Christian movement into institutional churches and perfectionist sects was inevitable. The same kind of process was inevitable for The Salvation Army. Should we Salvationists then focus our thinking on how our movement can recover the movement mentality that gave it the spiritual vitality and missional passion that made it so fruitful for the Kingdom of God in times and places past? If so, then how?

Deep in our hearts do we not know the starting place for this recovery? And is it not to return to where and how the Christian movement began in the first place: to follow Jesus and allow Him to free us and teach us to become *His holy, radical disciples*? The New Testament makes it clear what this means:

* having Jesus' heart **(II Corinthians 3:1-3; 4:6; Galatians 4:6; Ephesians 3:16-19; Philippians 4:7; I Thessalonians**

3:13; II Thessalonians 3:5; Hebrews 10:16; I Peter 3:15);

- acquiring His mind (**Romans 12:1-2; I Corinthians 2:16; Ephesians 4:20-24; Philippians 2:1-5; Colossians 3:16-17**); and

- living in the world by the priorities and values of the Kingdom of God He inaugurated (**Luke 12:31; Romans 14:17-18; I Corinthians 4:20; Ephesians 5:5; II Thessalonians 1:3-5**).

We must then ask and find answers to the question: How can our corps nurture and resource holy disciples who see their entire lives as a mission, their lifestyle as Kingdom-of-God-specific, and their gifts as assets for mission (service, evangelism, and discipling)?

To answer this question, let's take a closer look at the nature of a movement. (I am indebted to missiologist Alan Hirsch for expanding my understanding of Christianity as a movement that evolved into an institution, and for his proven ideas about how the church can reclaim its character as a missional movement.) It is the nature of most committed movements that, like their founder, are deeply concerned about those who are not its members. Movements tend to arise with a growing concern for the outsider, the others who are excluded from the benefits of those who are insiders or more privileged. In the more extreme cases, the others may actually be dehumanized, exploited, or persecuted people.

Christian movements follow a similar pattern. They are

- *deeply committed to Jesus* (**Matthew 4:18-22; Mark 8:34; Luke 9:23; John 8:31-32; I Peter 2:21**);

- *motivated by compassion* (**Luke 10:29-37; John 3:16; I Corinthians 9:22**);

- *empowered and guided by the Holy Spirit* (**John 14:26; Acts 1:8; chapter 2; I Corinthians 12:7-11; Ephesians 3:14-19**); *and*

- *won over by an inclusive Gospel* (**Luke 1:52-53; Acts 13:44-47; Romans 3:29-30; 15:7-12; Ephesians 2:11-16; 3:14-15**).

They are comprised of disciples who are wholeheartedly given over to Jesus and to those outside the church, and especially to those who are marginalized (**Matthew 25:40; Luke 13:29-30; 14:1-6, 12-14; 18:9-23; 23:39-43**).

Some movements within the church fall short because they lack a key essential to a truly Christian movement. They may seek a spiritual renewal or revival without an expression in compassionate outreach. Consequently, they suffocate on the confined air of their excessive self-attention. Or another movement may be so obsessed with reaching out to the spiritually lost, or feeding the hungry, or helping the marginalized in other practical ways, or fighting social injustice that they starve themselves of the spiritual food, even of the love and prayers of the Body of Christ. Eventually they die from lack of spiritual sustenance and connection with the church whose support they so much need. Healthy and ultimately effective Christian movements spend time together in worship and prayer, shared confession, and mutual accountability. They also and especially are drawn together by their compassion for the lost, the hurting, and the abused. Both dimensions of their discipleship—their communion with God and each other and their commitment to mission—form a union that makes for authentic disciples. They cultivate their deep love for Jesus, and they spread that love like seeds thrown across the landscape of their world. They cultivate both spiritual depth and missional breadth. They are true Christian movements. Open to each other and to where Christ is taking them.

Facing the challenge of keeping the Salvationist movement alive

The house churches of early Christianity allowed for both the intimate spirituality and the outreach of witness and service. The Wesleyan bands and societies, as well. The early Salvation Army often worked through groups called brigades. At their best these brigades combined spiritual growth and service outreach.

It is my observation, however, that over time these two aspects of discipleship were increasingly separated programmatically. Today, Bible studies, for example, are often taught in a kind of vacuum in which Scriptural concepts are conveyed but direct implication of the Word for individual participants' life and mission are not addressed and explored. A band or songster brigade may become very performance-oriented internally, but spend precious little time using their music in outreach mission or having members leave their music behind and visit hurting and forgotten people. Likewise, a corps group formed for personal spiritual growth and mutual support may confine their attention to each other and make little, if any, connection with their life in the world, nor hold up in prayer what each member faces each week, nor hold each other accountable for following his or her own specific calling. On the other hand, a corps group formed for a particular mission (evangelism, visitation, community service, advocacy, etc.) may lack the practice of Scriptural guidance, the habit of prayer, and the mutual encouragement and accountability so essential for their mission. Spiritual development and mission are of a piece. To make them separate programs is to create a spirituality without breadth and a mission without depth.

The institutional Army, like all institutional churches, is in danger of dividing and programatizing the individual parts of what needs to be an integrated Salvationist movement. Here are some examples of the split-ups:

- Evangelism and discipling become programs separate from each other, with the result that neither is usually done well. Conversions are counted and celebrated as stand-alones instead of being seen as what they really are—the doorway into the whole point of the evangelism: the making of disciples of Jesus. We make conversion a meaningless statistic when we fail to see it as the first step toward making disciples of our converts, and when we fail to let our converts know what they have actually gotten themselves into. The purpose of salvation is nothing less than sanctified discipleship!

- Social outreach and spiritual witness are each pursued apart from the other in order to keep our social work pure—*i.e.*, disengaged from spiritual issues and acceptable on its own professional merit—and our spiritual witness equally pure—*i.e.*, not contaminated by the messy social dimensions of a person's life. Such a dualism is a violation of the Bible's holistic view and is therefore a heresy in practice.

- Any separation of Bible study groups, discipling groups, and mission or service groups divides the life of a Salvationist into separate spheres, weakening each of them. Bible study should be more than a pursuit of Biblical knowledge; it should be the textbook and marching orders for both discipling and mission. The discipling of Salvationists should be based on Scripture and tested and assessed in the person's life lived out in the world (mission and service). Likewise, the mission or service of the Salvationist must surely be guided by Scripture and enabled by discipleship training.

These programmatic divisions are very typical of institutionalized churches. They weaken the movement mentality by breaking up the indivisible and segmenting our lives. None of the programs are bad in and of themselves. They are ministries worth doing. In a particular corps any one of them may be done very well and serve a real need. The problem is that all too often we see them as separate activities in our corps and fail to integrate them to shape the holistic life and mission of the corps. Sometimes they are done to satisfy certain program standards, their real mission thereby lost sight of.

In Chapter Seven we will consider specific ways a corps can be reshaped by a movement (our original) mentality. For the present, it is worth our thinking and praying about how our own corps may have diminished or even lost the missional focus of a movement of disciples. Then we can begin to think about how we personally and our corps as a whole can start

to turn the ship at sea toward becoming a missional movement heading in the right direction. Once we launch that process in our corps, we will start discovering who we are as a missional people and deciding who we are as a Salvation Army. We will find the deep joy of answering Christ's call to join the Christian movement He founded and still leads.

FOR REFLECTION & PRAYER

Which Scripture verse or passage in this chapter spoke most deeply to you, or challenged you most? Say why.

Christianity: a movement that became an institution

Personal: Do you personally see your corps as primarily a place to go to or as a place to be sent out from? What does your answer teach you about how you see your calling as a disciple?

Your corps: Describe aspects of your corps that suggest a movement, and then describe aspects that suggest an institutional church or a perfectionist sect? What do your descriptions say about your corps?

Keeping the Christian movement alive

Personal: What can you personally do to help you become more a disciple of the Jesus movement rather than a member of an institutional church or a perfectionist sect?

Your corps: Which of the following aspects of discipleship would you like to see strengthened in your corps? How specifically might that aspect be strengthened?

- Deepen members' love for Jesus
- Strengthen the compassion of Jesus in members' lives
- Help members be guided and empowered by the Holy Spirit
- Grow members' commitment to mission

Facing the challenge of keeping the Salvationist movement alive

Personal: What thoughts might you have about how you personally could round out or complete your life as a disciple of Jesus by giving full attention to an area you feel you have neglected?

Your corps: What thoughts might you have about how your corps could better treat discipleship, worship, Bible study, and mission as an indivisible whole?

CHAPTER 7

RE-IMAGINE YOUR CORPS AS A MOVEMENT

Your paneled houses
are blinded and neat;
but the souls that sing on
will have following feet.
Surrender your ceilings!
A deluge will come,
And the down-pour will drown out the
life-giving Troubadour Song.
His Kingdom is coming:
It starts in the street.
It is built in the hearts
that have following feet.
Let it sing in your heart.
Don't look over your shoulder,
But run to be one
In the army that come[s]
to march with the Son
to the sound of the drum
that will beat with the heart
of the Troubadour Song.
(Andy Raine, *Celtic Daily Prayer, Book Two*, p. 1471)

Those raised with Christ remain gladly dependent on
God's Spirit in every move they make in the world as
witnesses, in the Church as members, and in the clos-
et in prayer. (Markus Barth, *The Broken Wall*, p. 74)

Is it possible for our Salvation Army, highly organized and departmentalized denomination that we now are, to retain or regain the spirit of a mobile movement? Can it still be focused on a world in serious trouble, rather than its own preservation, procedures, and promotions? Can a corps—your corps—become drawn like a magnet more to engagement with the world than to the comforts of its own corps fellowship. In sum, can your corps look more like a movement following Jesus into the communities where the corps is situated and also into those where members live? Or is our witness now confined to a corps building as the only place where members are able to express their Christian faith and service?

I believe that without a return to the former ways called for by the Old Testament prophets (see, for example, **Malachi 3:4**) and repeated in the New Testament to churches who had abandoned the world-embracing Gospel of Christ (see, for example, **John 3:16-17; Acts 15:12-18**), we will become something safe, gradually diminish, and eventually die. This return to the former ways is neither a repetition of the exact practices of the past nor the automatic repetition of traditional programs. Those practices and programs grew out of the missional mentality of past days given the nature and needs of the communities we were trying to reach. In their day they were not prescribed formulas or inherited methods. They were Spirit-inspired new responses to the current realities of the mission field.

The early Salvation Army, with Spirit-inspired insight, made things up along the way as it risked following what it believed the Spirit was saying to the church. We honor our amazing forbears, not so much by continuing their methods and programs as by imitating their courage and Spirit-reliance in forging new paths and taking new risks for the gospel in the specific world where *we* are in mission.

I am not proposing terminating Army programs just because they have been around for a long time. I am proposing, first, that we consider no program as sacrosanct if it is not concretely advancing the mission of our corps and does not engage the people we are trying to reach. If the program cannot be adapted to serve our mission, it should be considered as not worth the time we are spending on it.

I am proposing, second, that responsible, prayed-for mission experimentations should be encouraged and supported. This is a recommendation to free corps and corps officers, in consultation with DHQ, to exercise the missional creativity and courage that made this Army so successful as an evangelical movement in its earlier days. (I remember a corps officer who had started a very effective addiction recovery and support ministry in his corps, leading to a number of conversions, disciplings, and even some soldier enrollments, being told by DHQ that there was no place to record this ministry. It didn't conform to the program categories of the corps statistical printout! Presumably, therefore, it could not exist as far as our organizational structure was concerned!) It is not hard to see how missionally ridiculous it is for corps programs to be dictated from the top while successful new experiments that are accomplishing our mission are ignored and not supported. The Salvation Army was built on new ventures and risky experiments in mission!

Third, I'm proposing that we place the greater emphasis on every Salvationist's witness when he or she is *not* at the corps

(Acts 1:8; Colossians 4:5-6; Hebrews 13:13-16; I Peter 2:11-12). The Lord takes great delight if a corps has a missional mentality in the way it approaches and conducts its programs and ministries. His greater delight, however, is for the corps to prepare and equip its member to live the life of Jesus in all the communities where they spend the other 90+ percent of their week when they are not attending the corps. What a solid corps is capable of doing in mission is considerable. What its members are capable of doing in mission outside the corps is extraordinary. The Kingdom of God, like salt, is most effectively employed when scattered rather than utilized as a lump **(Matthew 5:13)**. Since Christ "climbed up above all the heavens so that He might fill everything" **(Ephesians 4:10)**, we can no longer confine Him to our corps and its programs. He is everywhere, and we must seek Him everywhere. Every Salvationist should ask the question: How well is my corps preparing me to live the life of the Kingdom of God for most of my week? If the answer is positive and it results in positive action by an increasing number of Salvationists, the corps' missional effectiveness will probably grow exponentially in the ways that matter most for the Kingdom of God.

Let me now invite you to reimagine your corps in three ways. First, reimagine your corps centered on Christ's mission. Second, reimagine your corps' mission guiding and governing its maintenance issues. And third, reimagine a comprehensive profile of your corps as a movement.

Reimagine your corps centered on Christ's mission

Think of our Army history. Corps were originally formed to be mission stations. The original intent for the Army to be an evangelistic agency, referring its converts to churches, largely failed. Most churches weren't interested in, nor were they equipped to handle, these converts from the lower urban classes. Many of the converts returned to the Army, an unintended consequence for which the adjustments needed to be made. If churches weren't willing or equipped to handle these new converts of humble means in their particular church family, the Army would. In fact, the Salvationists shaped a working class church culture where the very lowest social classes could feel welcome and at home. A chorus sometimes sung was:

> I'm at home in the Army
> more than I am anywhere.
> You can dress as you like.
> You can sit where you like.
> You're all quite equal there.

William Booth's claim that he had to begin with "a blank sheet of paper" is worth our remembering. It wasn't that there were no precedents for the radical steps the Army took to enter the world of the poor and working classes of Great Britain, with other countries to follow. As we saw in Chapter Six, the early church first made its greatest inroads in the poorest urban classes and the slave cast of the Mediterranean world before eventually becoming a power and status-based institution. Over the course of its history, other Christian movements have arisen, specifically to place their witness among the common people and the poorer classes— the excluded. Booth's hero John Wesley had himself made a momentous and much-criticized leap to bring the Gospel to the working classes of Eighteenth Century Britain. By the latter Nineteenth Century, however, the Methodists themselves had become more prosperous and largely out of touch with the now massive poor and working classes of the burgeoning industrial cities. The situation in the slums was desperate, poverty was rampant, and the poorer classes were disconnected from the churches. Booth set out to do what Wesley had done, but a far more industrialized Great Britain with sprawling slums required new measures.

We'll sum up those measures under two interwoven strands. We'll call the first strand *cultural adaptation*. It meant this:

- Locate corps where the poor and working classes live.

- Use the language of their culture.

- Use their music (popular tunes, some from the bars) and their mobile media (brass bands, flags, marching).

We'll call the second strand *incarnational holiness*. It meant this:

- Live among the poor and working classes.

- Respond to their concerns and needs in helpful, empowering ways.

- Be Jesus to them, and present Jesus to them.

Similar kinds of adaptive, incarnational measures were time-tested over almost nineteen centuries of Christian movements that came into being to reach previously excluded people groups. But Booth's measures differed in that the state of British society and its urban slums in particular was historically unique. No mimicry of previous approaches would do. The strategy needed to be specifically suited to the reality of the lives of those the Army came into existence to reach for Christ. It was by this evangelical compulsion that Booth's blank page became occupied with a flood of fresh ideas which were soon shaped into the Army's missional covenant.

In light of this missional covenant to be a people called especially to the excluded, *how do you see your own corps?*

First, consider your corps *location.* Is it located in a poorer part of the city? If it is, how well is it doing relating to the everyday lives of the neighborhood people? What percentage of your corps congregation is comprised of these neighbors? In what ways is the Christ who is present in the neighborhood inviting your corps members to join Him there in doing what He is trying to bring about in people's lives—spiritually, socially, and physically? How can corps members "be Jesus" in the neighborhood?

If your corps is located in a largely middle-class neighborhood, how might it reach those in the community who have no Christian faith or affiliation? (Avoid the temptation to lure existing church members—that is, to recirculate Christians!) If there are pockets of poverty in proximity to the corps, how can your corps become an intimate part of those more passed over communities? If there are no poorer communities nearby, what further removed, more marginalized community could your corps commit itself to be more personally involved in on a long-term basis.

Second, consider *how best to live the life of Jesus and bear witness to the Gospel in the neighborhood of your corps' missional focus.* How do you first come to understand the real issues and concerns of the people in the community? How do you resist the temptation to jump to your own conclusions about the neighborhood before you spent time there as a learner? How then do you trust the Scriptures enough to believe that the Gospel speaks to whatever the neighborhood's needs and concerns are? If you then have patiently come to understand the neighborhood's hopes and fears, will you study, pray over, and trust Scripture to guide your mission?

If your corps is willing to take these two major steps, it is in a position to become the kind of missional force Jesus called us to be and the early Army modeled for us. To do this, however, your corps will need at the same time to address its own internal life and activity. Your corps will need to:

Reimagine its mission permeating and guiding all aspects of its internal life

Think about your corps. If mission is truly its priority and if the congregation is truly healthy and inclusive, then the chances that the corps will grow in a solid way are good. (By "solid" I mean growth that is not based on artificial gimmicks, which alone do not bear real harvests.) If, on the other hand, keeping the programs going and the machinery running take precedence over mission, it is almost certain that the corps will decline and eventually die. The Salvation Army in the Western world (including the USA) has overall been declining for decades. We've been trying hard to hold our own, stop the decline, double our efforts in largely doing the same things over and over, perhaps with minor surface changes or different titles. In some corps soldiers and officers are wearing themselves out trying to keep all the standard programs going. Other corps live in an atmosphere of perpetual dissatisfaction because their purpose is not clear. Still other corps are comprised of long-term soldiers who, for the most part, enjoy each other's company and are happily growing old together as a (closed) corps family. All these corps are dying. Only the healthy missional corps will prosper both spiritually and numerically.

It is nevertheless true that every missional corps does require good internal maintenance. Officers and soldiers alike are stewards of corps ministries and resources, and weak programming and management do not help a corps carry out its vital mission. Nor does the claim of a strong missional passion excuse settling for incompetent programs or sloppy administration, on the mistaken notion that management responsibilities detract us from mission. In reality, without competent programs and diligent management of resources, a corps' mission, begun with enthusiasm and met with early success, many flounder because it grows beyond the corps' capacity to sustain. The reasons for the failure may be any one or more of the following:

- Lack of a long-range plan or the following through with one

- Lack of mission team meetings for updates, assessments, prayers, and mutual support

- Lack of needed leadership development

- Insufficient leadership from volunteer corps members (rather than paid corps staff)

- Little or no investment in garnering sufficient support and prayer from the corps congregation

- Lack of periodic reports to the corps congregation

The only way to avoid those pitfalls is good management of the mission. Without it, any number of bumps in the road may wreck the already weak support system for the missional initiative. For example, a change of corps officers always comes with some disruption. Sometimes the disruption is helpful. The new corps officer may be exactly what the corps needs. On the other hand, the new corps officer may have his own program preferences, and if the previous mission initiative is poorly organized and not well sustained, it may not survive the newly arrived preferences.

Beyond this need for good management overall, is the even more important issue of *what* a corps is managing. Sometimes a corps is well-managed and -maintained but stagnant or declining. One must ask why that is. There may be a lack of spiritual outreach, a spirituality seeking personal blessing for the gathered few only. Or there may be outreach programs with a lack of real spiritual depth. A true spirituality develops disciples of Jesus who devote themselves both to their own growth as followers of Jesus and to their calling to go into the world to serve others and make disciples. This is what we earlier called holiness full measure.

The most important first question of corps management and maintenance, therefore, is: *What are we managing and maintaining?* Are we managing and maintaining activities that are advancing our calling? Does our oversight give priority and require accountability for the mission for which our corps and its programs exist? In short, does our mission guide and govern our management? Maintenance without a mission focus leads ultimately to death, spiritually and numerically.

We come back, then, to the matter of how a corps can be a movement focused on mission rather than an institution focused on itself. Let's think about how your corps can:

Reimagine itself as a movement

What would a movement corps look like? What would be its characteristics?

First, *a movement corps (like any true movement) is deeply committed to the calling and teaching of its Founder.* For any Salvation Army corps, that Founder is Jesus Christ. He is the way, the truth, and the life (**John 14:6**). His journey is the corps' journey (**Matthew 4:19-22; 9:9; Mark 1:16-20; 10:28-31**). His truth is the corps' truth (**John 1:14, 17; 8:31-32; 15:26-27; 16:12-15; 18:37; Ephesians 4:21-24**). His way of life is the corps' way of life (**John 8:12; Romans 6:1-4; Ephesians 5:1-2; Colossians 2:6-7; I John 1:7; 2:5-6**). As He is holy, so corps members are called to be a holy people (**Ephesians 1:4; 5:25b-27; Colossians 3:12-14; I Peter 1:15-16**). As He gave His life for the world, so corps members are called to do the same (**Matthew 16:24-25; Mark 8:34-35; Luke 9:23-24; John 3:16; 10:11; Romans 12:1; II Corinthians 1:5-7; 5:15-21; Philippians**

3:10-11; Hebrews 12:1-3; I Peter 4:12-16).

Second, *a movement corps is called to unity in all things* (**John 17:17-23; Romans 12:3-8; I Corinthians 12:12-26; Ephesians 4:1-6; Colossians 3:14**). This doesn't mean members agree on everything. It means that in all they do, the members seek to serve the purpose for which the corps exists. Everything the corps does serves the mission. For example, in your own corps it would mean:

- *Worship*: As a corps we worship not only to praise and glorify God on a Sunday but also to equip us to do the same in our lives in the world (**Romans 12:1-2**). We worship not only to be blessed but also to carry blessing to others during the week. We worship to seek a holiness that is not only personal but also social, lived out in the world (**Ephesians 5:8-20; I Thessalonians 5:4-8; I John 5:1-5**). Worship and mission are one and the same service.

- *Bible study*: As a corps we study Scripture not only to enlighten ourselves and grow spiritually as individuals, but also to receive our Lord's instructions and commands as to how to live our lives in all the communities where we live during the week (**Psalm 119:105; Luke 24:44-49; II Timothy 3:14-17**). The Bible, the Word of God, is aimed both to change our hearts and to send us out.

- *Prayer*: As a corps we pray both for ourselves and for the world. Too often, corps prayer, as well as private prayer by Salvationists, is focused on the needs of corps members and their families and friends (whom we want to and should be praying for) but derelict in including the needs of the larger world (neighborhood, city, nation, all nations and ethnicities) and for the success of Christ's mission both near and far (**Matthew 5:43-48; 6:9-10; Luke 6:28; 10:2; John 17:15-19; Acts 13:1-3; II Thessalonians 1:11-12; 3:1**). Prayer must take us beyond ourselves and our own needs. It must expand our boundaries to include the whole world!

* *Discipling*: As a corps we are disciples who take our discipling seriously by responding to how the Holy Spirit is seeking to shape and grow us as disciples through worship, Bible study, prayer, holy living, and giving ourselves for the world (**Psalm 24:3-6; Isaiah 2:3; Malachi 3:3-4; Matthew 4:19; 19:21; Luke 4:8; John 8:31-32; 10:27; 12:26; 15:5-8; Acts 2:42-47**).

* *Mission*: As a corps we are all called to mission. Our worship, Bible study, prayer, and discipling prepare and equip us for it (**I Kings 8:59-60; Isaiah 55:11; Matthew 6:9-13; 13:23; Mark 4:20; Luke 8:11-15; 28:16-20; Mark 8:6-7; Acts 6:4; Acts, chapter 10; Romans 15:30-31; 16:26; Colossians 3:1-10; I Thessalonians 3:12-13; II Thessalonians 1:11-12**).

Whatever the current state of your corps' spiritual and missional health, you can begin to see steps that could be taken toward a more spiritually strong and missionally centered body of believers. You can have conversations and prayers with other corps members who also long for a spiritual life with depth and outreach with breadth. Your corps may already have strengths to build on, or perhaps your strengths are few. Simply begin where you are to build a vibrant Jesus movement—which is to say, a real corps, a corps passionate about the mission of Jesus and united in sharing His good news with the world.

FOR REFLECTION & PRAYER

Which Scripture verse or passage in this chapter spoke most deeply to you, or challenged you most? Say why.

Reimagine your corps centered on Christ's mission

Personal: Consider how you can best live the life of Jesus and bear witness to the Gospel either in the neighborhood of your corps or in one of the neighborhoods you inhabit during the week. Describe what this mission would look like.

Your corps: Describe a step you think your corps could take better to center itself on Christ's mission.

With whom could you helpfully discuss your thinking on the matter?

Reimagine your corps' mission permeating and guiding all aspects of its internal life

Personal: Is there any aspect of your own corps involvement that you would like to be more missionally fruitful? If so, what step might you take to make your involvement better serve the mission?

Your corps: Is there a way you think the overall management and operation of your corps could better serve its mission? Please describe.

Reimagine your corps as a movement

Personal: What could you do personally to recover for yourself the movement mentality of the New Testament church?

What could you do personally to recover the movement mentality of the early Salvation Army?

Your corps: As the unity (not uniformity!) of the corps in all things is so essential to its mission, where might your corps need to do work to achieve the needed cohesion of a true Salvationist movement?

Who are the leaders of your corps with whom this can be helpfully discussed and effectively addressed?

CHAPTER 8

REUNITE WORSHIP AND MISSION

*The people gathered to hear from Christ, to let Him
dwell in their hearts, to follow His call—this is the
worshiping assembly... We note specifically that their
worship follows no fixed rule except this one: that it be
worship in which Christ officiates, in which His death
and resurrection are accepted as the saving and revealing sacrifice, and in which His Spirit is not resisted. This
worship has no limits. It is not an affair of one hour of
one day a week only, or of special seasons, or of people of
certain social standing or race, or of the feeling, the
mind, the bodily presence only. The worship to which
Paul calls the Ephesians is enjoyment of an open access
to God wherever they walk.*
(Markus Barth, *The Broken Wall*, pp. 190-191)

*The Christian engages in worship in order to clarify the
action he must take in everyday life, to reinforce his spirit
so that he becomes a coworker with the God Who is at
work in human affairs.*
(Frederick Coutts, ed., *The Armoury Commentary—The
Four Gospels*)

In the previous chapter we said that God calls our corps to
worship not only to praise and glorify God on a Sunday but
also to equip us to do the same in our lives in the world—or as
Barth put it in the opening quote, to enjoy "an open access to

God wherever [we] walk." The purpose of the present chapter is to show why this integration of worship and mission is so crucial for any corps that fulfills its calling.

The early Salvation Army did not seem to be generally fond of the word worship. This was partly due to the fact that we began as an evangelistic agency and not a church. It was also because even after we became a church home to many of our converts, the word worship was associated with a cultivated Christianity whose worship neither appealed to nor related to the world of the urban poor. There was little joy and scarcely a sense of freedom in much church worship. The joy of salvation and the freedom of expression were therefore to become important hallmarks of Salvationist worship. So, the Army didn't call its religious gatherings worship; they were called meetings!

Meetings were seen as a means to an end. The largest meetings were Salvation Meetings, the purpose of which was to get people saved. As these meetings aimed to attract large crowds for better evangelical fishing, they had more the flavor of entertainment so as to draw the people in. The smaller meetings were Holiness Meetings, the purpose of which was to get the saved sanctified and growing in holiness. Their character was more introspective. The success of all meetings was largely measured by how many people came forward either for salvation or for holiness.

True worship is not a means to an end that worship planners calculate as the expected outcome. The Bible calls God's people to worship God for who He is and for what He has done. The very word worship implies that the One who is worshiped determines the outcome. In the Old Testament the most frequently used Hebrew word to designate worship of the true God (*shachah*) has the sense of bowing down and doing obeisance (**Psalm 95:6-7**). In other words, though the one bowing down may have his own ideas of what he hopes the outcome of this worship of God may be, it is God Himself who determines it. The most frequently used word for worship in the New Testament (*proskuneo*) has a similar sense (**Matthew 4:10; Revelation 22:9**), with the added dimension that *Jesus* is also worshiped (**Matthew 2:11; 9:18; 14:33; 28:9; Luke 24:52; John 9:38**).

Worshiping in this Biblical way, "in spirit and truth" (**John 4:23**), will bring all kinds of Kingdom of God outcomes: people will be saved, sanctified, and healed; prayers will be answered; prophetic voices will be heard and obeyed; and a host of other gifts from God will be given at one time or another, in one way or another, in one place or another. If, however, our worship is planned and led with only *our* predetermined outcome in our minds, we are trying to manipulate God, and He may have something far different or better in mind. The important thing in worship is that we come to it expressing our love for God, our faith in Christ, our confidence in the Spirit's leading, and with a willingness to be changed. Of course, we come to worship with our own personal expectations and hopes. God will gladly take them, sift them, and come up with the best for His Kingdom and the best for us. It may be more, or less, or something entirely different from what we expected.

Along with the gradual acceptance that our Army is a church in the New Testament sense, has come a growing desire to discover true worship. Sometimes we do it well; sometimes not. What we may not have come fully to realize is that we have one huge advantage in our approach to worship, and it seems to me we rarely seem to employ it. We will come to that later, but first let's take an honest look at some issues concerning our worship.

Some concerns with current Salvationist worship

I have observed and participated in Salvationist worship over a long period of time. Many were the times I felt that God was not only present but also speaking and acting. There were other times, however, when I sensed that something other than true worship was taking place, or that there were elements in the service that distracted from genuine worship. I hasten to add that I have conducted no formal study of the matter; this is only my opinion based on observation. Furthermore, some of what I describe may not seem to you to be as inconsistent with true worship as I do. I only ask that you read with an open mind, as I have tried to do in my own assessments.

My first concern is a tendency for some Salvationist worship meetings to seem to emphasize *entertainment*. This has roots in our early history when our evangelistic meetings had to have a draw and a way to keep the otherwise un-predisposed to pay attention. There are still types of Army gatherings having worthy purposes that have little to do directly with worship. And, in fact, worship itself is and should be greatly enhanced by music (**I Chronicles 15:16; Psalm 33:1-4**), visual representations (**Numbers 21:9; Psalm 20:5**), and dance (**II Samuel 6:14-15; Psalm 149:3**). When it come to our Holiness meetings, our weekly worship as the Body of Christ, however, there should be no room for casual humor, flashy technical displays, or the injection of any stimuli merely for effect. (Incidentally, I still frequently hear the order of our worship referred to as a program, which carries the sense of entertaining an audience and suggests the service is in the hands of the planners and leaders, rather than God. Could we agree to give up that term for lent, as well as forever, as a reference to worship?)

Along with the emphasis on entertainment, is the quest for a certain kind of *experience*. The media world in which we live is a manipulative empire that has become adept at creating appetites for a huge diversity of experiences with little concern for the true value or authenticity of those experiences. We have become an experience-seeking culture. In such an environment, the temptation in planning and leading worship is for us to use various and sundry means to manufacture spiritual experience in general or a specific kind of spiritual experience in particular. In worship there should be no need for emotional manipulation or tricks to predispose worshipers toward a decision they would not otherwise make. Worship is an encounter with God, and from that encounter—not our programmatic manipulations—comes an authentic worship experience.

Another concern with some of our worship is what we might call *tribalism*. The Salvation Army is one tribe among other Christian tribes. Sometimes we are so concerned with doing things, including worship, the Army way that we fail to learn what other Christian tribes can teach us, as we can also teach them. We can even appear to worship all things

Army and condemn fellow Salvationists for departing from the peculiarities of our tradition. We truly honor the worship traditions of our Army, not by replicating every historic detail, but by opening ourselves to the Spirit's leading today, as did our forebears. Army worship is not a tribal cult to protect; it is a movement of the Spirit to expand.

Army worship can also fall victim to *perfectionism and excessive introspection.* To some extent this is due to our holiness tradition, especially certain extreme forms of that tradition. I am often surprised at how quickly we are invited to become introspective in Holiness Meetings. True worship must certainly begin with God, His praise, His goodness, His sacrifice for our salvation. It should not begin with us, our needs, our confessions, our guilt. The Gospel truth is that not until we see and hear God do we really *know* ourselves as we are and as God wants us to be, and we certainly don't know our real needs, our real sins, and our real guilt. It is God who reveals ourselves to ourselves. To open worship with an introspective song like Herbert Booth's "Before Thy face, dear Lord," for example, or even to sing it earlier in the meeting— all before we have heard God's story, sought His face and His grace, and placed ourselves at His feet in adoration—gets us too quickly to our psychological guilt feelings (not the same as real guilt) and feeds our drive toward an unhealthy perfectionism. This song has an appropriate place in our worship: when the time for response has come.

Related to this concern is another: *excessive individualism and privatization.* We come *together* for worship on a Sunday morning. It is a community event. Most invitations or commands to worship in the Bible are addressed in the plural.

"Come, let's worship and bow down! /Let's kneel before the Lord, our maker!" **(Psalm 95:6)**. "Bow down to the Lord/ in His holy splendor! /Tremble before Him, all the earth!" (*Psalm 96:9*). Much has been said about the decline of community in the modern world, and particularly in the Western world. This has been fueled by an individualism gone mad, driving people into private enclaves of self-concern and isolation from people who are outside their own close family and friendships. Our private worlds have become more important to us, and our social worlds have become far more selective. I wonder how much of this self-centeredness we now bring into our worship.

To begin with, there are a very large number of songs in our *Song* Book written in the first person singular. They certainly have their place in worship, but we would do well to be attentive to how and how often they are used in worship, which, as we've said, is a community event. I'm amazed at how often our prayers in Holiness Meetings revolve around ourselves, rarely branching out beyond our corps congregation. Yes, of course we should pray for the needs of corps members and their relatives, but if our prayer circle is only that small we are failing to follow Jesus into the world He loves and died for. Furthermore, if we were to enlarge our prayer circle, we may begin to see some of the things we pray for in our corps family as the petty requests they might be.

Approaching our worship as a community event in which all who are present participate leads us to another extremely important truth: As we worship as one Body, so also do we respond as one Body. No Salvationist worshiper should consider himself excused from the decision to move forward in his spiritual journey. Worship should be planned and led with the understanding that *everyone* is called to respond. Yes, there may be one or two persons present who are in the midst of a major spiritual struggle who, if they respond, may stand out in that service. But any Christian worth his salt will recognize a new way he needs to take, or a new decision the Spirit is calling him to make, or a new act of grace he could initiate. Otherwise, he isn't listening. The Spirit wants to move everyone in that worship gathering, as He did at Pentecost. In worship God is shaping a holy *people*.

Salvationist worship and the call to holiness

A corps is called to be a Kingdom of God community. It is called to live under the sovereignty of God the Father, follow the Lordship of Christ the Son, and find the unity of love in the Holy Spirit **(Ephesians 4:1-6)**. The life of the Trinity actually shapes the life of the corps, molding it into a holy people. Earlier in the book we discussed holiness as the way of life of the discipled and discipling corps. We now give our attention to how worship helps to build a holy community.

First, we can say that worship helps to shape a holy people when it has the three key subjects of Scripture: *God, His people, and the world*. Worship must begin with God: His person, His love, His word, His will, and His way. It must address the people of God, calling them to prayer, unity, discipleship, holy living, and love for one another. And worship must call the people of God to love the world as Jesus did and to give their lives for its salvation. Worship that does not include all three dimensions will fall short of shaping a holy people.

Second, worship helps to shape a holy people when it is aimed at *nurturing a community of disciples.* Most of Scripture was written to a community of God's people. A corps congregation is a band of disciples gathered around Jesus, allowing Him to script them as His holy Body. Worship is not for private individuals who just happen to be together for worship. It is for shaping a holy community of sold out disciples who are on a spiritual journey together. To this end the faithful reading and preaching of Scripture to and for everyone present is essential to true worship.

Third, this means that worship must be a *corporate act of humility.* Corporate humility may sound like an impossibility. How can we expect that everyone present in a worship meeting come in humility? We can't. What those who lead worship *can* do is make clear that God has called this people together in worship both because there is something He is calling them to be and do as a corps body and because there is something in particular He is calling each individual person to be and do. He doesn't call the whole body to worship only for the sake of a few members who presumably are the ones who need holiness. No person present in worship is called to be a spectator, as if he were there to watch what God needed to do in someone else's life, or what he thought that person needed to have done. He is called to participate in humbling prayer, to bow in penitence before God so that God can do what He knows that person needs in his journey in holiness. True worship destroys pride and humbles us all, and in doing so, opens us to the Holy Spirit.

Fourth, worship helps to shape a holy people when it is a *preparation and practice for the coming week.* As we bring the previous week to our worship in order to express gratitude for the Spirit's leading or confess our failings to God, so we also look forward to preparing ourselves for the opportunities and challenges of holy living ahead. In a very real sense, worship is practice for the coming week. Unfortunately, worshiping Salvationists sometimes disconnect their corporate worship from the realities of their individual lives, almost as if worship is meant to be an escape from reality, a relieving removal from the pressures of the week. The result can be a disembodied spirituality that is no help to living the life of Jesus in the world.

Indeed, we can and should rest in the Lord. Retreat and refreshment *is* a part of worship. But it must not be seen as an escape from the world and the mission to which we have been called. Quite the opposite; it is an essential part of our disciple life in the world. We retreat in order to gain perspective, regroup, and plan again for the war; we refresh ourselves in worship in order to return fresh for warfare. Worship participates in mission and is essential to it. We do not refuse to act like Christ-for-the-world Salvationists when we worship. True Salvationists know that worship is also mission. That is why, when we say the benediction, the Christ who has been in our midst in worship now takes His place at the door of our corps, inviting us to take our worship with us.

The corps at worship—everywhere!

Earlier in this chapter, we looked at the most often used Hebrew word for worship in the Old Testament (*shachah*) and the most often used Greek word for worship in the New Testament (*proskuneo*), both of them having the similar meaning of worship as bowing down or paying obeisance to someone. There are two other less frequently used words in the New Testament which have a related but more expanded meaning. It is the more expanded meaning that I think is a key to something new that is taking place in how Jesus the Christ is calling His disciples to be in the world. The words are *leitourgia* (meaning: service, ministry, worship, or offering, sacrifice), from which we get the English word liturgy, which means the order of a worship service, and *latreuo* (meaning: service, worship). These two Greek words tie our worship and our service together. They move out from the confines of an actual worship service to include serving others (**II Corinthians 9:12; Philippians 2:17, 30**). Especially noteworthy is the use of *latreia* in **Romans 12:1 (NRSV)** to describe the "living sacrifice" that Christians are called to make as their "spiritual worship." The verse that follows makes it clear that the apostle Paul is referring to the whole of Christians' lives, which are not to "be conformed to this world, but...transformed by the renewing of [their] minds, so that [they] may discern what is the will of God—what is good and acceptable and perfect" (**Romans 12:2**). Worship and service are of a piece. The giving of ourselves in worship is the giving of ourselves to the world for Christ's sake. A living sacrifice.

The early Salvation Army did not worship in places consecrated by established churches. They worshiped in unconsecrated theatres and street corners, consecrating these places not by ecclesiastical fiat but by missional fire. They followed a God who was at work everywhere and anywhere. Their worship matched the character of the environment, making holy what seemed common. They did not escape back to a sanctuary for protection; their sanctuary was at the gates of Hell where they worshiped with settled courage. A living sacrifice.

Consider Matthew, Mark, and Luke's account of Jesus presiding at His last meal with His disciples. This is worship, and when we consider the full witness of the Gospel accounts around this event, we see worship in full. Jesus gives thanks, shares the cup of His poured out love with His disciples, and then breaks the bread of His body, soon to be broken for them and for the world. It is a meal associated with Passover worship, which brings to remembrance God's intervention for the salvation of His chosen people. It takes place, not in a synagogue, but in a borrowed guestroom on a second floor somewhere in Jerusalem. John's Gospel gives us considerable further detail about what happened in connection with the meal. Jesus begins with an act of humble service: He washes His disciples' feet and tells them they must do the same. He teaches them about their future following His death and resurrection, His relationship with the Father, the Father sending the Holy Spirit to them as Jesus' continuing presence, their ongoing relationship to Him as the branches of the Vine, the hatred they will encounter because of their relationship with Him, and the certainty of His conquest of the fallen world. Then He prays for them. And let's not forget that in all four Gospel accounts, the betraying sin Judas bears in his heart is identified by Jesus. In Luke's account a deplorable argument breaks out over which of them is the greatest, and in John's account Jesus exposes the unreliable heart of Peter (**Matthew 26:17-35; Mark 14:10-31; Luke 22:7-38; John, chapters 13-17**). Plenty there needing forgiveness.

Here is worship: not only the gratitude to God, Jesus' sacrifice for the world, sin calling for confession, and the promise of the future, but also prayer for Jesus' disciples who will now be called upon to live the life of Jesus and carry His saving love into the world. Worship always has a commissioning, a sending out, as when the resurrected Jesus in His last appearance lifts up His hands and blesses them, and they respond in worship. He then commissions them to make disciples of all nations, and overwhelmed with joy they return to Jerusalem to begin the living out of their world-encompassing discipleship, assured that their Lord will always be with them. (**Luke 24:50-53; Matthew 28:16-20**)

Worshiping God and living the life of Jesus in the world are of a piece. We bring our lives into worship, and we bring worship into our lives. We tread on holy ground every day, wherever we are. We mark it as such by our holy living then and there. Albert Orsborn put into a song that has become a Salvationist treasure:

My life must be Christ's broken bread,
My love His outpoured wine,
A cup o'erfilled, a table spread
Beneath His name and sign,
That other souls, refreshed and fed,
May share His life through mine.

(*The Song Book*, No. 610, v.1)

The apostle Paul tells the Colossian Christians to do whatever they do, and say whatever they say, in the Lord's name and with thanksgiving, as if they were worshiping right out in the open (**Colossians 3:17**). Similarly, to the Ephesians Christians: "speak to each other with psalms, hymns, and spiritual songs; sing and make music to the Lord in your hearts; always give thanks to God the Father for everything in the name of our Lord Jesus Christ; and submit to each other out of respect for Christ" (**Ephesians 5:19-21**). Is this worship or daily Christian living, or both?

The writer to the Hebrews speaks of the importance of Christians worshiping together. "Don't stop meeting together with other believers," he says. "…think about how to motivate each other to show love and to do good works…encourage each other" (**Hebrews 10:24-25**). As worship is a part of our daily living, so our daily lives must be brought to our worship. Worship must be grounded in reality. In the love of the Father, under the Lordship of the Son, and by the leading of the Holy Spirit, we share our real stories. We encourage and motivate each other. We love each other.

Not long ago Keitha and I attended a Sunday morning worship service at one of our Adult Rehabilitation Centers (ARC) where Stephen and Donna were the pastors and administrators. We always find worship at ARCs to be quite moving because those who have hit the rock bottom of a life of addiction seem especially poised to understand and receive the grace of God. On this particular occasion, the service included the celebration of those beneficiaries who had reached the nine-month mark of sobriety. We were there to support Jay, a son of friends Allen and Esther. He was one of those who was being recognized for reaching that mark.

If I have ever heard powerful praising and thanksgiving, I heard it that morning, led by an in-house musical group that lifted the sanctuary rafters. If I have ever seen a congregation humble themselves before God and surrender to His sufficiency, I saw it that morning. If I have ever heard heartfelt testimonies of God's grace, I heard it that morning, again and again as each sobriety celebrant was invited to share his story. If I have ever heard our need for fellow brothers and sisters in Christ to get us through, I heard it as one man after another named fellow beneficiaries, family members, and staff members as the hands of God that got them through. If I have ever seen a group of people of different races, educational levels, and stations in life leveled into one family of equals, I saw it that morning. And if I have ever seen clearly the real issue for each member present, I saw it there. The real issue was the helplessness of every person gathered in that chapel—those with addictions and the rest of us for whom sin tempted differently—without the saving and sustaining love of the Father, found in Christ and available through the Holy Spirit.

Did any of us feel diminished by this recognition of our helplessness without God? Not at all. Stephen and Donna had invited Allen to preach. For his text Allen chose **Mark 2:1-12**, a story set in Capernaum, where four friends of a paralyzed man are so desperate to get their friend to Jesus in spite of overwhelming crowds around the place where Jesus was staying, they climb up on the roof, bringing with them the mat carrying their friend. They then proceed to lift enough tiles to get themselves and their friend inside.

Of course, this outrageous act causes a sensation. What does Jesus make of the rude interruption? He sees only one thing: the incredible faith of four friends, and because of it He says to the paralytic, "Child, your sins are forgiven!" It seems He is not healing the man's paralysis. He is addressing his heart, the real center of the man's life. The experts in Jewish law who are there jump in immediately to condemn Jesus for presuming to do what only God can do. Calmly, Jesus assures them He does have the authority, and then addresses the man on the mat, "Get up, take your mat, and go home." And he does.

The story seems tailor-made for what the ARC ministry is about—and what worship is, as well. We come together to glorify and praise God for who He is and what He has done on our behalf. We recognize our helplessness and our need of His grace and healing. We gather with fellow Christians because we need each other's help for our journey, companions who understand something of what we are going through and whom we can help on their journey as well. Whatever our presenting problem or struggle—be it addiction or some other manifestation—the deeper sin must be recognized and forgiven. We humble ourselves so God can actually do something for us. And we seek the Spirit's power and wisdom to help us release the love of Christ in the days ahead and live in the sobriety of a holy life.

Allen closed his message by continuing the story as he imagined it. The former paralytic goes home to greet his mother, who has until that moment seen her son only by looking down. Now, for the first time she has to look up to see him.

When you meet Jesus and allow His saving and healing grace into your life, said Allen, no one can look down on you and you can't look down on anyone else. You are on the way to becoming what God created and redeemed you to be.

It seems to me, that is what God wants us to know and carry with us when we leave Sunday worship to serve and worship Him during the week. Gratitude to God, dependence on His grace, reliance on the love and support of fellow travelers, humility before others, and confidence to live your calling. The Christ we worship does this for us. But we don't leave Him in the sanctuary following the benediction. We bring the sanctuary with us in our hearts and in our living. Our mission is the extension of our worship. Our lives become the living embodiment of His praise, His holiness, and His love for a world for which He gave His life. This is what the Christ who stands at the door of our corps reminds us as we depart.

FOR REFLECTION & PRAYER

Which Scripture verse or passage in the chapter spoke most deeply to you, or challenged you most? Say why.

Some concerns with current Salvationist worship

Personal: Do any of the concerns about Salvationist worship today that were addressed in the chapter reveal an area where you feel you need to grow in your own approach to worship? If so, what step could you take to grow in this area of your worship?

Your corps: In what area do you think your corps' worship could improve? How can you help?

Salvationist worship and the call to holiness

Personal: This section discusses a number of ways our worship can help to shape a holy people. Say which one relates most personally to you, and what you might do to grow more in holiness through worship.

Your corps: What step(s) in worship could your corps take in order to challenge and help all corps members at worship to grow in holiness? ,

The corps at worship—everywhere!

Personal: What can you do personally to relate your own worship to your life calling and your mission/service in the world?

What specifically can you do to carry your worship into your daily life and to make your daily actions an act of worship?

Your corps: What can your corps learn about worship from the ARC service described at the end of the chapter?

What changes would you like to see and with whom can you helpfully discuss this?

PART THREE:

THE MISSION
CHRIST INVITES US OUT TO BE
HIS MISSIONAL PEOPLE

Jesus came near and spoke to them

"I've received all authority in Heaven and on earth. There-

fore, go and make disciples of all nations, baptizing them in

the name of the Father and of the Son and of

the Holy Spirit, teaching them to obey everything

that I've commanded you. Look, I myself will be with you

every day until the end of this present age."

— Matthew 28:18-20

CHAPTER 9

MAKE DISCIPLES

*When the Church is taken merely as a means to trans-form society, very little is accomplished. For in that case the uniqueness of the Church is denied and we enter the battle on the same terms as secular and god-less forces. We assume the battle for right and justice can be won by force, by technique, by doing. It can't. These very clearly are not the weapons of Christian warfare (**Ephesians 6:10-20**). Truly Christian trans-formation of culture comes through Christlike (and hence sacrificial) love, community and being.*
(Howard A. Snyder, *The Community of the King*)

In Chapter 3 we pointed out that every Christian is called to be a disciple of Jesus, a "little Christ," an imitator of Jesus. We also dealt with various barriers to this calling that needed to be overcome and even eliminated. We talked about ways in which both new converts and undiscipled soldiers and adherents could be discipled in your corps. We now turn to an extremely important, and in fact indispensable, part of every disciple's calling: to *make disciples*. Disciples must disciple.

This may scare some of us. We may feel inadequate for such a responsibility. Aren't there other Salvationists who are especially experienced, trained, even gifted for this min-istry? Yes, there are. Some leaders have a unique calling that includes providing the corps with authoritative teaching about Christian faith and living. There are also leaders who have the gift of teaching. Why not leave the discipling to them? They are able, prepared, and ready. They're the real professionals.

Don't leave it to the pros!

Why not leave it to the pros? Well, because behind this view that only people with certain gifts can disciple someone is the assumption that discipling is cerebral and knowledge based. It takes place in a classroom or in some other controlled setting like a retreat. This approach tends to separate discipling from real life. It assumes that if we get it in our brains, the living will follow. Let's assume, for example, that a person being discipled in such a setting learns that Jesus calls him to love the unlovable. So, the diligent student says to himself, "I'll just start doing that."

He discovers it isn't so easy. There's really a lot more to learn about how to love the unlovable, not so much in his head as in his heart, his discernment, his actions. He will soon realize he is on a learning curve for which his head knowledge is not sufficient. He will make mistakes and must learn from them. Hopefully, he will discover that he still isn't perfect and that issues both outside and even within him complicate his ability to follow Jesus in this specific way. What is happening here, if he allows himself to see it, is that his limitation or failure is actually providing a real-life discipleship teaching opportunity for the Holy Spirit! If we refuse to admit that we're having trouble with living the Jesus life or if we revert to a pretended discipleship, then we will have abandoned a key requirement of being Jesus' disciple: the sincere desire to keep growing and learning (**Ephesians 4:15; II Thessalonians 1:3**).

The best way to keep growing and learning as a disciple may well be not to sign up for another discipling course. The best way is probably to talk with a fellow disciple you trust, or perhaps to be a part of a group of Salvationists sharing their journeys of discipleship with each other, supporting one another, sharing wisdom, and praying for one another. The group could be a Bible study group that approaches Scripture, not only to inform the mind about matters of faith, but also to perfect the heart and improve holy living. The growing disciple can bring their own personal challenges to such a group. Disciples helping disciples.

See your corps as a group of disciples on a journey together. Of course, each Salvationist is gifted for a specific role, and the use of all these individual gifts contributes to the overall journey your corps is on. All of us, however, contribute to each other's growth as disciples. We learn from what we see, hear, and receive from each other, as well as from what we realize others receive from us.

I am not ignoring the reality that all corps will have members or attenders who are not seriously pursuing discipleship. There are also those who have been Christians a long time and have stopped growing or are stuck in a past era of their lives and haven't moved beyond it. For all intents and purposes, they may be spiritually dead. Also there may well be a few who are psychologically or socially dysfunctional. My experience tells me it is unwise and unfruitful to focus primarily on changing them, as we are often tempted to do. If they are to change for the better, they must be motivated to change, and the best way for us to encourage that desire is to model a healthy, growing disciple life and to encourage them to be a part of it, to the extent they are currently motivated or ready for it. Love them, but don't indulge them or allow yourself to be manipulated or intimidated by them. All disciples are called to help others on their discipleship journey and also to be helped in their own development as disciples. We do this as a spiritual family. We not only share our progress, we also share our struggles in following Jesus. We also pray for one another and hold each other accountable. This is how our discipling takes place: disciples relying on one another, each part of the Body of Christ essential to the other, members sharing love, wisdom, and honesty. It's a lifelong journey we walk together, trip-ups and all, "until we all reach the unity of faith and knowledge of God's Son... and become mature adults...fully grown, measured by the standard of the fullness of Christ" (**Ephesians 4:13**). That's what discipleship is all about, fellow Salvationists, and to aim at something else is to miss the mark. The accountability to one another is really important. By "speaking the truth with love [to one another], we grow up every way into Christ" (**v. 15**). We disciple each other. We become like Jesus together. Discipling is a community affair, not a solo flight. The Christ who stands at the door of our corps beckons not just two or three specially-gifted Salvationists to disciple the rest of the corps; He invites us to disciple each other.

We're sent out to disciple

You will remember that when our resurrected Lord sends out His disciples just before His ascension, He commands them to make disciples (**Matthew 28:19**). That is the center of His disciples' missional calling. One territory summarized the Salvationist's mission as *loving inclusively, serving helpfully, and discipling effectively in all the communities where the Salvationist lives his life.* All three facets are part of one whole. They describe the disciple life. Loving inclusively is how disciples share the all-encompassing compassion of Christ. Serving helpfully is how disciples minister in ways that empower others as Jesus did. Discipling effectively is how disciples intentionally help others actually become and grow as disciples of Jesus. It's all our mission, and it's the mission of all of us—and we do it wherever we are in all the communities where we live.

When Salvationists are living the love of Christ daily, they are overcoming all manner of barriers of exclusion (**II Corinthians 5:14-19; Ephesians 2:14-16; I Thessalonians 3:12-13**). They are probably surprising people around them who live by those barriers, and they may find themselves ostracized by some of those who are walled in by their fear. They may even pay a heavy price for touching the lives of the excluded, as did Jesus and all those over the centuries who have lived by His radical compassion. Some, however, will notice, be deeply affected, and drawn in. Such a way of life is essential to being a disciple, and it is an indispensable goal of our Salvationist mission.

When Salvationists are serving others helpfully, they are refusing to pursue any course that would weaken or disempower other persons (**Mark 5:18-20; John 8:1-11; 13:14-15**). Jesus calls us to serve others in the same ways He did. We do this by helping people become stronger, move their lives forward to a better place, gain the strength to make better choices, and pursue a truly fulfilling life. Unfortunately, some charitable work is manipulative, an actual preying upon people under the guise of compassion. Other charitable enterprises actually serve to weaken people and reinforce the cycle of dependency. Such counterfeits of true helpfulness are not of Christ and deserve no place in our mission. Our calling as helpers is to enable and empower.

When Salvationists are discipling effectively, they are not only discipling one another as in the early Jerusalem church (**Acts 2:42-47**), they are also carrying out a mission to disciple all nations (or ethnicities) in the name of the Father and the Son and the Holy Spirit and to teach this whole world to pursue the life Jesus lived (**Matthew 28:19-20**). The heart of our mission is discipling, not our own good works. The good we do, the love we give, the help we provide is all the expression of the sanctified heart of a disciple of Jesus. We do not do it on our own; we do it through the Holy Spirit sent by Jesus, the Spirit that brings Jesus to us and empowers us to live like Jesus, even be Jesus.

If we are real disciples of Jesus, we love in a way that excludes no one. We serve in a way that empowers those we help. And we disciple effectively in everything we do by demonstrating how to live in the Kingdom of God and by assuring those around us that they can enter this Kingdom and discover the real Jesus for themselves.

All Christians are called to live the life of Jesus in the world. We are called to a "worldly holiness," a holiness lived out in the face of and alongside the world's un-holiness. Unworldly holiness (unchallenged holiness) does little, if anything, for the Kingdom of God. Holiness engaging the world is the holiness Salvationists need to be teaching and modeling for each other, supporting, praying for. Not many people without a religious faith are thirsting for theology from Christians. Many of them are thirsting for life in all its fullness, which is what Jesus came to give us (**John 10:10**). So, let's give it to them! The time for doctrine will come. The great challenge for us little Christs is to be like the Jesus who walked this earth wherever we are.

So, what does this mean for what happens in your corps? Perhaps a lot of things happen in your corps already. Perhaps there's too much of it that detracts from the real bottom line. What is essential is for Salvationist disciples to gather in prayer for one another, yes for personal needs, even more importantly for one another's life in the world as credible little Christs. We need to bring to our corps gatherings our experiences—successes and failures—as disciples of Jesus who need support from the whole Body and Bride of Christ. And we need some mature Christian leaders (the corps officer[s] and others) who can give wise counsel and loving support.

The Christ who stands at the door of our corps knows all of us, knows the potential and the abilities of each one of us. And He calls the whole lot of us to live like His disciples—inside and outside the corps—influencing others in Christ-positive ways, luring some to the way of Jesus, evoking an openness to faith, creating a beginning appetite for holiness.

Discipling before conversion?

The decline of Christianity as a broadly accepted foundation for life in the Western world—otherwise known as the weakening of Christendom—raises the question of how this shift may have affected the way we evangelize and disciple. We have typically seen evangelism, which aims at conversion, as the first step, and discipling as the second. For many centuries in the Western world, evangelism has relied and been premised upon a Christian culture. The person to be evangelized may have been the worst sort of sinner, but it was highly likely he had absorbed certain Christian assumptions from his culture if not by an earlier involvement in a church. Or he may have been a professing Christian and member of a church but had abandoned the church and fallen from grace. Either way, the evangelist could assume there was something of a Christian influence or knowledge or experience which could be appealed to, something inside the person with which the evangelist could find resonance. Or, the person could have intellectually accepted the truth of the Christian faith but had not crossed the line to become a serious follower of Jesus. Hence, the evangelizer's task was to push for a decision toward which the potential convert may already have been leaning or predisposed.

To the extent that we have entered what many call the post-Christian era, this approach to evangelism is decreasingly effective. The truth of the Christian faith is assumed or accepted by a shrinking number of people in the West, even though the majority still seem to have some belief in a God or a higher being, vague as it may be. Do we, then, approach them with rational arguments designed to change their minds so that they become ready to make a decision to follow Christ? Or does this place undue emphasis on intellectual assent as the starting point? Can a person so easily jump from intellectual assent to commitment of his life to following a Lord with such radical demands as Jesus makes? And if we emphasize the importance of conversion without the new convert realizing what following Jesus actually entails, do we set him up for failure because he didn't fully realize what he was getting into?

We seem to be entering a different world where the approach of evangelism first and discipling second is decreasingly effective. Or have we actually been here before? Consider Jesus' ministry. It primarily consists in describing what it means to live in the Kingdom of God. He doesn't call first for an evangelistic decision; He outlines and models a very different way of life, and He invites people to live that way. He doesn't make an evangelistic appeal; He leaves it to His listeners and observers to decide. In fact, He is cautious about those who respond too quickly for the wrong reasons (**John 6:26, 60-67**) or before they grasp what He's asking of them. He tells His intimate circle of disciples of His coming suffering, and they are clearly not ready to accept such an outcome in the life to which they thought He had called them (**Luke 18:31-34**), and when His suffering death does come they are unprepared, huddling in fear behind closed doors (**John 20:19**). There are also times when the crowds are taken in by Jesus' spectacular miracles, but their conversion proves to be only an inch deep (**John 2:23-25**).

Consider what happens at Pentecost (**Acts 2**). "Pious Jews" are gathered in one place in Jerusalem following the death and resurrection of Jesus. We don't know if they have already become followers of Jesus, or even know much about Him, but all of them, in a real sense, are on a journey of holiness and holy living. In other words, the discipling has already begun. At Pentecost the sanctifying Holy Spirit suddenly descends upon them with fire igniting them and wind clearing their minds, and the Spirit Himself so filling them they understand each other's speech even though they speak different languages. While onlookers jeer, they ask, "What does this mean?"

It falls to the apostle Peter to answer. He explains how this was all foretold by the prophets, and he recites the story of Jesus. Then he tells them that what they have just experienced is the pouring out on them of the Holy Spirit that Jesus had promised. The whole crowd realizes that something momentous has happened. Frankly, they're a bit unsure of where all this is supposed to lead. Many of them are afraid. What now? What shall we do? they ask Peter.

Peter is quick to answer: "Change your hearts and lives. Each of you must be baptized in the name of Jesus Christ for the forgiveness of your sins. Then you will receive the gift of the Holy Spirit. This promise is for you, your children, and all who are far away." Those who respond to Peter's message are then baptized—three thousand that day! And the discipling continues (**vv. 42-47**).

Clearly those who are gathered that day ("pious Jews") are already on a spiritual journey, some familiar with Jesus or intentionally seeking to follow Him; others not. The Twelve are definitely present, as well as others who have been following Jesus for some time. All of them, we could say, are on a journey in holiness, and to all of them Peter gives the invitation to "change [their] hearts and lives [and] be baptized in the name of Jesus Christ for the forgiveness of their sins." Having done this, they will "receive the gift of the Holy Spirit." For most, if not all of them, the discipleship began before this moment of Christian conversion. Their discipling will, of course, continue, but it started before Pentecost. If the church was founded on that day, it began with people from all over who were already seeking to live their lives as God's people.

Consider the letters of Paul. They are written to specific Christian churches or to regional groups of churches. The purposes and details of each letter vary according to the needs of the church(es) addressed. But all of them contain sections on doctrine and practice, theology and ethics. The doctrine is often foundational for the issues of Christian practice dealt with in the letter. We could say that these two sections correspond to the two dimensions of discipleship training, sometimes referred to as orthodoxy (correct belief) and orthopraxis (correct practice or behavior). The orthopraxis is our witness, our lure, as we "shine like stars in [a] world" that is held captive to deception and corruption (**Philippians 2:13-16a**). Disciples of Jesus are beacons of hope who demonstrate and recommend the freedom and joy of the kingdom of God. Just by *being* disciples in the world they are influencing others toward Jesus' way of life—they are discipling!

When we look at later New Testament letters, we see a very strong emphasis on disciples of Jesus living a life radically different from the behaviors around them. Clearly it was this faithful discipleship, this Kingdom of God living, that not only set the Christians off from everyone else, but also attracted those who saw this way of Christ being lived out before them as the life God intended for them. In other words, the credibility of how those disciples lived in the world was crucial for drawing others to Christ. The records of that day abound with both ridicule of Christian behaviors and deep admiration precisely because those behaviors were a stark contrast to current social norms. The beauty and grace of Christian living drew people into the Christian circle, where they were able to meet Christ, Who was the cause of it all.

The first letter of Peter is a good example of the emphasis in the early church on living the life of Jesus faithfully in a pagan culture that cannot connect with it or even accommodate it. Peter reminds his readers that as those who "share the divine nature" their lives must reject "the world's immorality that sinful craving produces" **(II Peter 1:4)**. Such a life is characterized by faith, moral excellence, knowledge, self-control, endurance, godliness, affection for others, and love—all of which they continue to cultivate in their lives, keeping them active and fruitful **(vv. 5-8)**. Clearly, living the life of a radical disciple of Jesus in that world was not a way of life that could be kept hidden or quiet. It sent a strong message and was all the more effective because it was done with humility and grace by those who were for the most part socially and politically powerless. In the pagan culture of the Mediterranean world, the way to draw people to the Christian faith was to live it straightforwardly with courage. It was the living of Christians—the undeniable authenticity of their discipleship--that drew people in. People wanted the joy and authenticity of this new way of life. In this sense, the disciple living of one group was the evangelical lure to another group.

Over the centuries there have been other missional settings, places where Christianity was relatively unknown, where the credibility of the life lived by Christians was the real battle-ground and test of Christian authenticity. For example, think of Christian missionaries seeking to evangelize ethnicities who worship other gods. If Christianity is declining in our Western world, the credibility of Christians and of the lives they are living is more than ever crucial in drawing that world to Jesus. People are more drawn to Jesus because they see Him in our lives than because they are convinced by our doctrinal propositions and arguments or by our emotional appeals.

Jesus calls all His disciples to go and make disciples. Salvationists have historically taken that calling seriously. Follow Me, says Jesus, and I'll bring you in and teach you to be a citizen of the Kingdom of God, and My Spirit will empower you to live by the law of this Kingdom. It's called the law of love, it's called holiness. It's what makes it possible for you to be My disciple.

Jesus teaches us that this life, this holiness is a thing untamed by social convention. It pulls and compels us out into the world, where the Kingdom of God is actually located. It's largely hidden, but it's waiting for disciples crazy enough to trust its presence and actually live by its strange rules; a holiness largely countercultural.

Mission is how disciples of Jesus live their lives in the world. It's show-and-tell all over the place. Show the world our feeble, though sufficiently credible living. Show them a God who really does "so love the world that He gave His Son" to save it. Show the world and *tell* the world. Talk, talk, talk—like Peter and John saying, "We can't stop speaking about what we have seen and heard" (**Acts 4:20**). Talk in normal conversation, with an awareness that God is present in the conversation, with the Holy Spirit giving you openings and words, eye contact and pauses—and ears, for actually listening to the other person.

And gradually, or suddenly, we start realizing that we are actually discipling someone toward faith, inviting someone to enter the Kingdom of God, and then walking further with them. This is discipling in the world where we actually live. We are discipling with our lives. This is what every disciple of Jesus, every Christian, and every Salvationist is called to do.

Christianity has suffered from its misrepresentations in today's world—spirituality parading as personal prosperity, church leaders treating congregations as their own kingdoms, professing Christians living double lives—to mention only a few of the counterfeits. What is needed more than anything is for you and me to live the life of Jesus, be disciples, follow Jesus *wherever we are.* Then some people may want to be like us, may even start imitating us. They may not know it at first, but they will have begun a journey toward Jesus and a new way of life.

Jesus invites our entire corps to live in the world so convincingly as His disciples that some people will want to be like us, some will even start acting like us, until they see Jesus and embrace Him as Lord.

FOR REFLECTION & PRAYER

Which Scripture verse or passage in the chapter spoke most deeply to you, or challenged you most? Say why.

Don't leave it to the pros!

Personal: In what specific way(s) could you see yourself helping someone else in your corps develop as a disciple of Jesus? What would you need to do to begin, and who might you begin with?

Your corps: What could your corps do to encourage and facilitate mutual discipling among Salvationists?

We're sent out to disciple

Personal: As you live the life of a disciple of Jesus in your daily life in the world, how could you better begin to draw someone toward and into Kingdom of God living? Answer in at least one of the following areas of your life:

Family

Workplace

Neighborhood

Friendships

Your corps: How could your corps better prepare corps members for such discipling? And how could members be held accountable for this essential part of their mission?

Discipling before conversion?

Personal: Name a particular person you know who is not a professing Christian but displays either a spiritual hunger or interest, or whose life and attitudes display hints of Christian values or compassion. As you share your life with this person, how can you affirm those qualities of his or her life that are consistent with the mind of Christ and the values of the Kingdom of God? As those attitudes, actions, and values are affirmed, how might you then discover the right way and time to give witness to Christ and seek to lead the person to faith in Him?

Your corps: How can your corps help you and other members to do evangelism in this way? Talk to your corps officer or other corps leaders about this.

CHAPTER 10

FIND OUR MISSION

*The person who dares not say an ill-natured word or do
an unreasonable thing because he or she considers God
as everywhere present performs a better devotion than
the person who dares not miss the church... To be humble in our actions, to avoid every appearance of pride
and vanity, to be meek and lowly in our words, actions,
dress, behavior, and designs—all in imitation of our
blessed Savior—is worshiping God in a higher manner
than do they who have only stated times to fall low on
their knees in devotion.*
(William Law, *A Serious Call to a Devout and Holy Life*)

*In many lands the churches have literally stolen
Christ from the people; they have taken Christiani-
ty from the city and imprisoned it behind altar rails*
(Henry Drummond, *The City Without a Church*)

The book *Servants Together* uses a practice from the Orthodox branch of Christianity as a metaphor to describe the role of
the Christian in the world (International headquarters, 2002,
pp. 28-29). The Orthodox Church uses religious paintings called
icons, not so much as something to look at but as windows to
see through to God. In our own Salvationist tradition, we speak
of our witness as our calling to reflect Christ, as when we sing
"Let the beauty of Jesus be seen in me." *Servants Together*
says that when we join the mission on which God sends us, we

become "living icons of Christ," commissioned by the Father and empowered by the Holy Spirit, mirrors reflecting and windows revealing God to the world.

I recently witnessed a total eclipse of the sun. It happened on August 21, 2017. We had traveled to Silva, North Carolina with a small group of friends where there would be totality for two full minutes. Thousands had come from far and wide to see this rare event. It was like a happy family homecoming, even though our group were total strangers to everyone else there. For a day, in a country divided, this stunning celestial event brought us together.

Whether or not we knew it beforehand, we discovered that we had come together to see transcendence. In a world where awareness of God is declining, or even disappearing, there is a deep hunger for something profoundly spectacular, holy, breath-stopping, something that overwhelms us with a sense of an awesome presence. For some who saw the total eclipse that day, there were no words, only a worshipful silence; for others, no explanations, only a quiet, mystical *aaaaah*; for other observers, no artificial self-control, only a very loud *whoa!* During this totality, the moon didn't so much obliterate the sun, it actually revealed the sun's glory: the corona that emanates from the sun into the universe, something we cannot see at any other time, now became luminous, sparkling streamers of crystal light, an indescribable glory surrounding the darkened moon's obstruction.

Here is perhaps another metaphor of our disciple witness in the world. Are we called so to align ourselves with God that we help people see His corona glory, His real nature?

Are we called to live in such a convincing way as followers of Jesus that we help to eclipse the world's blindness and distortions? Are we called to live our lives in such a way that because of us, people begin to see something of what God is *really* like with His corona glory of inclusive love and saving grace? Martin Luther said that Christians are called to be "little Christs." The apostle Paul said we're called to be "imitators of God" (**Ephesians 5:1**), reflectors of His light and His love in the world, all the time. And our Lord Himself said, "let your light shine before people, so they can see the good things you do and praise your Father who is in Heaven" (**Matthew 5:16**). Be living icons of Christ. This is our mission.

In this chapter we're going describe how we find our mission. First, we'll look at the *where* of our mission. Second, we'll look at the *what* and the *how* of our mission. And third, we'll consider the *margins* of our mission.

In mission wherever we are

With respect to holy living in the world, the Christian church faces two dilemmas. The first dilemma is that all too often it allows unholy motivations and actions free play in the church. It's not that unholy battles take place (they took place in New Testament churches as well!), it's that all too often they are expected as part of the normal course of church life, and therefore tolerated or ignored. The power of church leadership positions is too frequently abused; power driven leaders are often allowed to undermine the values of the Kingdom of God and exploit congregations for their own ends. Such unholy controversies and compromises will always take place this side of eternity, but to treat them as normal rather than unhealthy for the Body of Christ and not to confront them with prayer, sensitivity, and forthrightness, is to cripple the Body. If holiness is not nurtured and un-holiness dealt with in the life of the church itself, members will be ill-prepared to be holy disciples of Jesus in the world.

The second dilemma is that many professing Christians live in two worlds. One world is their church where they worship, sing and profess their faith in God, listen to preaching, tithe, learn and affirm their doctrines, meet and catch up with their church friends, and then leave to enter the other world they live in. An amazing transformation then takes place. Alan Hirsch describes the change this way: monotheists become polytheists, worshipers of one God become worshipers of many gods (see *The Forgotten Ways*, pp. 100, 105-108). To be sure, they may live that remaining 95 percent of their week as fairly respectable family members, friends, neighbors, employees, employers, and the like. However, they all too often worship at other altars. They may worship at the altar of the god of consumerism, defining their worth by their wealth and the acquisition of the best the market can offer (**Psalm 49:5-9**). They may worship at the altar of the god of their own ego, driven to undertake only those actions which serve their own interests (**Galatians 2:20; 5:22-24**). They may worship at the altar of the god of worldly success, obsessed by getting ahead, beating out others, acquiring a reputation, making it to the top (**Matthew 20:25-26; Mark 10:42-43**). They may even worship at the altar of their families, making an indulgent, smothering god of them (**Luke 14:26**). There are other such gods, as well. The point is this: There are many gods in our world, vying for our worship, tempting our allegiance with offers we may find hard to resist.

How, then, do we keep and nurture our allegiance to the God who will have no other gods before Him (**Exodus 20:3**)? The answer begins to come when we start at the right place: to see the world as belonging to God and Him alone (**Psalm 24:1 [I Corinthians 10:26]; 46:10; 47:7; 83:18; 89:11; Acts 17:24**). God through Christ has conquered the world (**John 16:33**) and taken captive the principalities and powers that have oppressed us (**Colossians 2:15**). And because of this conquest, we disciples live victoriously through our faith in Jesus the Christ (**I John 5:5**). The *real* God of our world is the God *over* the world, the God Whose Son was victorious on the cross, not defeated (**I Corinthians 1:18-25**), as validated by the resurrection (**Ephesians 1:20-23**). The world is the place where sin in all its human manifestations has been defeated.

So then why is sin still rampant? The answer can only be: because the victory succeeds only where it is accepted and lived, only where the crucified Jesus is received and followed as Lord. Saving love must be received and sanctifying love lived, and it is in the living that we find our mission in the world. Simply put, *our living is our mission.* Yes, our mission includes our participation in the outreach and service of our corps, and it also calls us to share our personal resources with the Army in parts of the world where poverty is rampant (World Services). But the most important location of our mission is the world in which each of us lives the rest of the time. The question all disciples must work through and work out is what it looks like for them to live in that world in obedience to Jesus and in disobedience to the other gods vying for our allegiance. This entails how we approach all our relationships, our family life, our jobs, our politics, our voting, our leisure—everything! Our witness is how we live our lives all the time.

The mission of Jesus' disciples is whole life mission. This does not mean, however, being uptight all the time, obsessive compulsive about putting an overt witness on everyone we see and blurting out testimonies in ill-timed moments and insensitive approaches. Such methods usually alienate and turn people off. More often, whole life mission means living a normal life, only in a way that reflects the compassion of Jesus and the values of the Kingdom of God. We need to be sufficiently Jesus-like in our daily attitudes and actions that people will take a second look and maybe get curious. In our day the authenticity of our Kingdom of God living—*i.e.*, our holy living—is the shape our mission takes.

Whole life mission requires a frontal assault on the heresy that divides the sacred world from the secular. The heresy is perpetuated not so much in our overt doctrinal statements and teaching; rather, it resides deep in our psyche as a sub-conscious principle we have learned by observation and experience. We have learned from others that when we leave church and enter the world, we have to operate by different standards in order to fit in, get by, look normal, and succeed. Living by this operating principle will kill our Christ-given mission more effectively than anything else.

God already resides in His totally conquered world. The Holy Spirit, the Spirit of Jesus, is present there to show us how to live in it as God's holy people. We stand with Wesley who had a strong doctrine of prevenient grace; the grace that goes before us. There is no situation we find ourselves in the world where God is not already present, and there is no holiness that is not "mobile," as Tennent says. Any location can become holy ground, a place where God reveals Himself and even performs a miracle. Our mission is to be a part and facilitator of it. The Salvationist's mission statement we referred to earlier in the book ends with the designation of the location of the mission to which we, all of us, are called: "in *all the communities* where we live." None of our locations excluded! Yes, the Jesus at the door calls us to the everywhere of our lives.

In mission whatever we do

In one of his most well-known poems, Robert Frost draws from an experience of chopping wood outside his rural New England home. Two woodsmen pass by, having just completed a woodcutting project with a lumber company. The woodsmen stop and exchange greetings with Frost. After some lingering they move on. Frost surmises they were hoping he would hire them to finish his job. Frost doesn't take the bait. He, the amateur woodcutter, is thoroughly enjoying what he is doing. The men are looking to make a little extra money. In the telling of this story, Frost leads us to see the beauty of work done for the love of it and the sadness of work done dispassionately only for subsistence or even survival.

An amateur is literally someone who undertakes a task out of love (Latin *amator* means lover). Frost concludes his musings with the unforgettable line: "Only where love and need are one...is the deed ever really done" (*The Poetry of Robert Frost*, "Two Tramps in Mud Time," p.277). If we approach our whole lives as our mission and every deed we do as a hint of God's love in Christ, a love the world desperately needs, then we are giving ourselves to the vision that everything we do affects our mission, and our mission affects everything we do.

The apostle Paul gives us his own unforgettable lines when he tells the church at Colossae how they are to do what they do as God's people. First, they are to clothe themselves with compassion, kindness, humility, gentleness, and patience. Then he invites them to be tolerant and forgiving toward one another. "And over all these things [they are to] put on love, which is the perfect bond of unity." Then he says to let the peace of Christ control their hearts, to be thankful, and to allow the word of Christ to live in them richly. Watch over each other and share wisdom, he says. Then top it off with a gratitude to God expressed through music and singing of all kinds. And finally, he sums it all up by saying, "Whatever you do, whether in speech or action, do it all in the name of the Lord Jesus and give thanks to God the Father through Him." (**Colossians 3:12-17**) In everything the follower of Jesus does, the deed is only done and the witness only given, when the love of Christ and human need meet. Disciples of Jesus are Christly lovers in what they do—whatever they do.

Holiness is love at work in everything we do. We are called to it wherever we Christ amateurs (Christ lovers) are at work, in all the tasks we undertake. This is why Paul talks about the Christian life as a walk. Note: The Greek verb Paul uses is *peripateo*, which literally means "to walk." Some modern translations helpfully translate the verb to mean "to live." Paul is being consistent with the Old Testament's use of the Hebrew word *halakh* (walk) to refer to the moral and spiritual life (**Psalm 119:1-3**). To look at the Christian life literally as a walk lends an everywhere-you-go specificity to our witness. We take our faith with us, always. Paul isn't talking about some kind of excess baggage we carry around with us as a display of our righteousness; he's talking about the way we walk, the way we do everything we do as "little Christs." He's talking about seeking with the Holy Spirit's help to live like Jesus as best we can in everything we do. We're never perfect at it, and we have to confess that sometimes we fail miserably at it. We may do it poorly here or botch it badly there. Then we confess our failure or, if need be, our sin, receive God's forgiveness and learn a new lesson in holy walking. If we have actually hurt another person by our insensitivity, we ask their forgiveness and try to heal any damage done by our falling short of holy love.

A sampling of the apostle Paul's uses of "walking" to describe the ways Jesus' disciples are called to approach everything they do is a rich collage of holy living. Salvationists can actually see them as their marching orders: walking in newness of life (**Romans 6:4c**); walking in the openness of day, not the secretiveness of night (**13:13**); walking in love (**14:15**); not walking by mere human standards (**I Corinthians 3:3**); walking consistent with the calling God has given us (**7:17**); walking without shameful deception or manipulation of God's Word (**II Corinthians 4:2**); walking by faith, not sight (**5:7**); followers of Christ walking together in the Spirit (**12:18**); walking in the Spirit so as not to gratify selfish desires (the flesh) (**Galatians 5:16**); walking worthy of our calling from God (**Ephesians 4:1**); walking in love, following the example of Christ (**5:2**); walking as children of light (**5:8**); walking wisely, not foolishly (**5:15**); walking in imitation of good Christian role models (**Philippians 3:17-18**); walking worthy of the Lord Himself and pleasing to Him in every way, and by doing so producing fruit in every good work and growing in the knowledge of God (**Colossians 1:10**); walking in Christ Jesus the Lord in the same way we received Him (**2:6**); walking wisely in the way we act toward outsiders

(4:5); walking worthy of the God who is calling us into His kingdom and glory **(I Thessalonians 2:12)**. John the apostle also uses "walking" to describe how we live the life of Jesus in the world: walking in the light of God, who is light **(I John 1:7)**; walking in the same way Jesus did **(2:6)**; walking in love **(II John 6)**; walking according to the truth **(III John 3)**. And Revelation looks forward to the day when all ethnicities will walk by the light of God's glory flowing from the lamp of the Lamb of God **(Revelation 21:23-24)**. And so we walk: toward, into, and throughout eternity.

The idea of a disciple's whole life as a walk requires that we take seriously both the mobility of holiness and our calling to be holy in everything we do. For the follower of Jesus there is no holiness that is here-but-not-there. Following Jesus means bringing Him into every personal and public relationship and asking Him to affect and maybe transform that relationship. The call to witness is given everywhere, with or without words, in or out of church. Jesus calls us to keep walking with Him.

In his second letter to the Corinthian church, Paul uses the language of an army at war to describe our mission. He says that even though we live in the world, we don't fight our battles with worldly methods (literally, "according to the flesh"). Instead, we receive a divine power to overcome big obstacles and demolish arrogant arguments—every opposition to the knowledge of God. And then the apostle makes a huge claim: We take every thought captive and make it obedient to Christ **(II Corinthians 10:3-5)**. This certainly doesn't mean we Christians out-argue those who disagree with us or are opposed to us. Christian apologetics does have its place; the church needs some Christians who can engage non-Christian intellectuals. But winning intellectual arguments will win few converts to Christ, because conversion is primarily of the heart. Intellectual arguments are not our primary weapons. Nevertheless, whenever someone asks us to speak of the hope we have in Christ, we must give a reason, we must be ready to tell our story and tell it well. The way we do it, however, is not argumentative, and certainly not belligerent. It is done "with respectful humility, maintaining a good conscience" (**I Peter 3:15-16**). The God "who reconciled us to Himself through Christ" has given us "the ministry of reconciliation," not divisiveness (**II Corinthians 5:18**). The world will be drawn to Christ by revealing the living Christ Himself, not by arguments won. We are the revealers, "little Christs" with a Bible in our hand and the world on our heart.

In mission on the margins

> I propose to go straight for these sinking classes, and
> in doing so shall continue to aim at the heart. If we
> help the man it is in order that we may change him.
> (William Booth, *In Darkest England and The Way Out*)

The true vision of the Old Testament is of a God whose heart is for the whole world He created, including all the places on the margins. The psalmist David declares that "the Lord's faithful love fills the whole earth" (**Psalm 33:5b**). Unfortunately, the chosen people of God sometimes forgot that this was a calling for them to reach out and give witness to all ethnicities (**Genesis 18:18; 22:18; Jeremiah 3:17; 4:1-2; Micah 4:1-4; Zechariah 2:11; 8:22**). Ironically, many in the church also fell into the trap of eliminating certain people groups, and sadly throughout our 2,000 year history this sin of exclusion has continued to plague us (see chapter 7). We have too often turned a deaf ear to our resurrected Lord's command to "go and make disciples of all nations" (**Matthew 28:19a**). Note: The New Testament Greek word usually translated as "nation" (*ethnos*, from which we get the English words ethnic and ethnicity) does not have quite the precise meaning that the word nation, meaning nation state, does today. It is perhaps more helpfully translated today as "ethnicity" or "people group." This understanding enables us to see the Gospel's inclusiveness aimed specifically at all ethnicities, whether or not they are identified with a specific nation state. It is especially helpful because the great majority of nations, especially in the Western world, have a multiplicity of ethnicities. Jesus' call to an inclusive mission points us, not only to other nations, but also—and perhaps especially—to a people who now live not far from our corps or our own neighborhoods, and probably inside our neighborhoods.

Drawing from Israel's history, the Letter of James is addressed to "the twelve tribes who are scattered outside the land of Israel," referring to the church dispersed across the Mediterranean world (**James 1:1**). As the scattered and scattering church, followers of Jesus are called not only to profess their faith but also to live it (**1:22-25; 2:14-17**); to welcome and honor the poor, show mercy, and resist favoritism (**2:1-13**); to tame the vicious, gossiping tongue (**3:1-10**); and the wealthy members are to resist hoarding their wealth and to treat their workers fairly (**5:1-6**). In this way the scattered and scattering church infects the world with Kingdom of God values by practicing compassion and living holy, and by breaking down prejudice, exploitation, and class divisions. The dispersion of credible Christians into the corners and crevices of the world is crucial to our mission. William Booth once called this Salvation Army "one vast missionary society."

The Gospel is borderless (**I Timothy 2:1-4**).

The Gospel is not only borderless, it's oriented specifically to the margins. The writer to the Hebrews emphasizes that the place where Christ suffered on the cross to make us holy was "outside the city gate," on the margins where no respectable person wanted to be. It is to this place that the writer invites us to go join Christ and "bear His shame." We disciples leave our Jerusalems of security and respectability, because they are not our true places of citizenship. We belong on the margins, where we are called to "do good" and "share what [we] have" (**Hebrews 13:12-16**)—Kingdom-living on the margins! The margins are the fertile fields for mission, as our early Army proved when it invaded the marginalized communities of the urban slums.

The margins are central to God's strategy to save the world. We see it in **Colossians 1:25-27** where Paul reveals God's "secret plan" (*musterion*, meaning mystery or secret) to the former outsiders and now included Gentiles, the plan which he later calls simply "Christ" (**2:2**)—Christ, the Savior of the margins. Only such a Savior can "bring all things together" (**Ephesians 1:10**) by including the outsiders. It must begin "outside the city gate" where those who "weren't a people" are now "God's people" (**I Peter 2:10**).

Our mission begins with Jesus Himself. We might ask: If He is the Savior of all, why did He spend most of His time with the poor and excluded, those on the margins? Did He not care for, was He not also sent to, people with more substantial personal assets and higher positions in the social and religious orders? They need saving, too! It is an important question. We could answer by pointing out that the poor constituted about 90 percent of the Palestinian population and therefore, on the principle of proportion, deserved the lion's share of Jesus' time. There is a measure of truth in this explanation. But I don't think it gets to the real heart of the matter. Call to mind Mary's Magnificat that begins with the mother-to-be of Jesus glorifying God for having chosen one of such low status as her to bear the Savior. She then goes on to describe what God was going to do through Jesus: He will show mercy to everyone, scatter the proud and arrogant, pull the powerful down from their thrones and lift up the lowly, fill the hungry with good things and send the rich away empty-handed (**Luke 1:46-53**). Throughout the Gospels, those who hold more power in the economic and religious structures of society usually don't impress Jesus and are frequent recipients of His stinging criticism (**Matthew 19:24; Luke 6:24; 12:15-21; 16:19-31**), and the early church followed His lead in cautioning against wealth's dangerous seduction (**I Timothy 6:9-10, 17; James 5:1-6**). The Letter of James criticizes favoritism shown by some Christians toward the wealthy (**James 2:1-7**) and in the same passage specifically designates "the poor as heirs of the Kingdom He [God] has promised to those who love Him" (**v. 5**).

Why are the wealthy and the religious leaders never specifically designated in the New Testament as heirs of the Kingdom? That must surely be because wealth and all positions of institutional power, including higher church positions, so often and easily become ends in themselves and lead to a sinful presumption of spiritual endowment and deserved blessing. The only way a person of high status can stand before Jesus, truly see Him, and then actually follow Him is for the person to allow Jesus to cut through the blinding exterior of privilege and power and expose the real person beneath it all for Jesus to work on. For many, that is a risk too costly to take, as it apparently was for the rich young ruler (**Mark 10:17-27**) and for quite a few Pharisees and Sadducees (**Matthew 16:6; 23:25-28**). The poor and marginalized usually find it easier to respond to Jesus because they have less to lose and see more to gain. Life is likely to have humbled them. It is certainly more challenging, however, for the highly placed and the powerful to find sufficient reason to humble themselves. Their assets are security, status, worth in the world. Some, however, do humble themselves, and Scriptures make clear again and again that this huge step must involve the end of hoarding wealth and clinging to status. Wealth must be shared generously, position taken off display and employed for the benefit of others, especially the marginalized. The prosperous grain merchant must stop building more barns and start sharing his grain with those in need (**Luke 12:15-21**), and the Pharisee named Nicodemus, a member of the prestigious Sanhedrin, must outgrow his pride of religious rank and become a new person through a spiritual rebirth (**John 3:1-21**).

The marginalized are key to Jesus' salvation project: If He cannot save them, then His salvation is not for all. And if the powerful cannot confess their sin and share power with the powerless, if members of the religious establishment cannot confess their sin of presumption and humble themselves before others, He cannot save them either. The poor and marginalized are absolutely key, not only to the success of Jesus' mission, but also to the mission to which we, His disciples are called. There is no more luminous display of God's corona glory, no purer and more penetrating revelation of Jesus, than when His disciples share themselves, their compassion, and their faith with "the least of these"—when they become "living icons of Christ."

Whoever the Christian group or congregation might be, their witness must meet this criterion. This is to say that their mission is inclusive of those on the margins, through either direct involvement or generous support, or both. A Christian church may be located in an upscale community and is committed to discipling these neighbors. In doing so they must be clear about Jesus' requirement that His followers share generously with the poor and seek their benefit and their salvation. The powerful cannot be disciples of Jesus unless they share their power with and actually *empower* the marginalized. Like their Lord, Jesus' disciples are a distinctive people of the margins.

From its beginnings The Salvation Army has located itself in the margins. Whether in our day a particular corps is geographically located among the marginalized or not, the hearts of its members must beat to the rhythm of inclusion. Those easiest to exclude must be the first to be included. Every corps in one way or another must reach the margins with saving and empowering grace. The Jesus at the door of our corps invites us out to find the least desirable places and the humblest people. How else can we prove that "whosoever will may come"?

FOR REFLECTION & PRAYER

Which Scripture verse or passage in the chapter spoke most deeply to you, or challenged you most? Say why.

In mission wherever we are

Personal: As you reflect on your own life, can you think of any way(s) in which there is inconsistency or conflict between your claim to worship God alone and aspects of the life you live in the world that may indicate an allegiance to other gods? How might this undermine your personal witness and mission? If so, who or what is that other god?

What step(s) could you take to address this? If you needed support in taking such a step(s), who could you reach out to?

Your corps: Can you think of a step your corps could take to help you and other Salvationists live in the world more consistently as Christian monotheists?

In mission whatever we do

Personal: Think of something you are passionate about, something you really enjoy doing with another person or other people. Can you see a way you could bring your Christian faith and discipleship into the way you do and share this activity with others? Describe what that might look like.

Think of something you are <u>not</u> passionate about but it is a job that you must do. How could you approach that job as a way to represent Jesus and convey His love to others?

Your corps: Think of a way your corps could be or is serving its community in some helpful and practical way. How could that service be done in a way that imitates and reveals Jesus, a way that goes deeper and builds a caring relationship with persons receiving the service, a way that better opens the door to a genuine witness?

Who in the corps could you partner with in exploring this?

In mission on the margins

Personal: Consider a person or a family living "on the margins" that you are aware of. If the Holy Spirit were to call you to represent and reveal Christ to that person or family, how could you begin?

What would be some of the obstacles (either on your side or theirs) you would need to overcome?

How would you begin to do so?

Your corps: Think about how open your corps is to people living on the margins. Is the corps congregation helping them in practical ways? How enduring are the relationships?

How welcome are they made to feel in the life of the corps?

Are they being evangelized? Discipled?

What step(s) could your corps take to be inclusive in the way Christ calls His followers to be?

CHAPTER 11

LIVE MISSIONALLY

*I now call upon all present to witness that I enter
into this covenant of my own free will, convinced
that the love of Christ, who died and now lives to
save me, requires from me this devotion of my life to
His service for the salvation of the whole world...*
(quoted from *The Soldier's Covenant*)

In previous chapters we emphasized that living as a disciple of Jesus requires an awareness that discipleship is a permanent and persistent calling. Or to use Salvationist terminology, salvation soldiers are always on duty. The apostle Paul uses the military metaphor to make an important point to his protégé Timothy: "Nobody who serves in the military gets tied up with civilian matters, so that they can please the one who recruited them" (*II Timothy 2:4*). In other words, Jesus doesn't recruit part-time disciples—though sadly some of His recruits seem wrongly to think He does.

Let's be clear, however, what full-time means. It's not as if God is spying on us to make sure we're not acting like mere "civilians" sometimes; not as if we'd better not put down our guard, relax, and enjoy life. Being super self-conscious of our every move, forever fearing we'll make a false step and do something un-disciple-like is not what our Lord is interested in. Our Lord came to give us life in all its fullness (*Ephesians 3:19*). To obsess over the correctness of every step is to make ourselves nervous and fearful Christians, shackled by an impossible, obsessive-compulsive legalism. Fullness of life in Christ means that the Christ who "fills everything in every way" (*1:23*) now dwells in us (*3:17*). This happens through the Spirit, who gives us an undeserved identity with Christ and the joy of eternal life (*Romans 8:9-11*). We carry this identity with us wherever we go and whatever we do. Some of us express that identity better than others, and all of us do it imperfectly. But we stay conscious of who we are. We pursue to be like Christ, not by keeping our noses to the grind and trying hard not to slip up anywhere, but by allowing the Spirit to purify our hearts and by obeying the Jesus who goes before us. The point is to live a *whole* life in Jesus, accepting both the happiness and the sufferings that come with following Him. The point is to begin by realizing that as disciples of Jesus, our calling is to reflect Him in whatever way possible, whenever and wherever.

To live this way is to live missionally. In this chapter we're going to look at some of the ways we do that. We'll look first at how we condition ourselves for missional living. Second, we'll look at how essential the corps congregation and other Christians—our support system—are. And lastly, we'll look at the ways we actually give our witness.

Condition yourself

We tend to see mission as something we do out there in the world. It is action oriented, and we Salvationists are known for our action. A missional life seen exclusively in this way, however, will fail. Mission is not primarily using Gospel knowledge we have acquired or a ministry skill set we have developed in order to give witness in the world and serve people in Christ's name. It is, first of all, bringing a relationship we have with Jesus to all our relationships in the world, and allowing Jesus to enter and transform those relationships. It is getting to know Him personally, and then being who we are in Him and doing as He does. In this section we will discuss the dimensions of a disciple's personal life that prepare him to live missionally in this way.

The first way we condition ourselves for missional living is through *solitude and prayer*. Too often we separate solitude and prayer from our mission: We may decide some of us are good contemplatives, others are good activists. Some pursue the internal life of solitude and prayer, others engage in mission. Scripture, however, gives us no liberty to choose only one or the other. We cannot choose between a prayer ministry and missional activism. Being a missional Christian, a true disciple of Jesus, means we are both contemplatives and activists.

No follower of Jesus can truly represent their Lord to others if they do not spend time with Jesus and in this solitude discover who they really are and what their calling is. Nor can a follower of Jesus isolate himself from the world and spend all his time praying privately and reading devotional books. True contemplatives are the best missional soldiers, and true missional soldiers are the best contemplatives. Contemplation alone is mere piety; mission alone is mere activism. Missional living is grounded in solitude (time alone with God) where we open ourselves to both the sanctifying and the discerning of the Spirit. The Spirit and the Word work on our hearts so that our minds can be clarified, able to see what Jesus is trying to do in us personally and what He is doing and still wants to do in the world. Together they empower us to allow Jesus better to live in our living and better to see Him and work in partnership with Him in the world around us. Missional living thrives and mission succeeds where this happens. Prayer and mission are meant for each other, and they produce fruit when they are married.

The second way we prepare ourselves for missional living is by *traveling light and keeping it simple*. Aidan, the great leader of Celtic Christianity in the Seventh Century, came from the aristocratic class, but as a bishop he refused to travel around on a horse, as befit his wealth and his status in the church. How could he speak of Christ to the common people standing by in the lanes if he was not on their level? He lived missionally by traveling light, and his mission for Christ thrived! Our Salvationist forebears lived and found joy in living by the bare essentials, and our mission thrived! Perhaps they remembered Jesus' words about the dangerous lure of wealth (**Matthew 6:24; 19:23-24; Mark 10:23-25; Luke 16:13; 18:22-25**) and His parable of the rich man having his life taken from him because he was rich toward himself rather than toward God (**Luke 12:15-21**). Perhaps they remembered Paul's testimony of contentment even in poverty (**Philippians 4:11b-13**) and his words to Timothy about this contentment with the bare essentials, the dangers of wealth, and the wisdom of the church not placing its hope in its financial prosperity (**I Timothy 6:6-10, 17-19**). Perhaps we Salvationists should ask if our Army has become so weighed down with material resources and external expectations we are now more like an establishment church rather than a missional church. And perhaps we should ask ourselves if we have allowed our own personal lives to be so distracted by consumerist drives and other multiple diversions that our witness suffers.

In a world of infinite complexity and diversion, Jesus calls us, His disciples, to discover the gift of simplicity. Emma Booth-Tucker, raised in the sparse environment of William and Catherine Booth's home, knew the meaning of the simple life. She knew what she was talking about when she wrote:

> Simplicity, parent of reality, offspring
> of sincerity, how great a charm!
> How unfailing an appeal to the heart of God! How
> invincible a weapon in the battle for souls!
> (*Heart Messages*)

How do we find this gift amid our distractions? In the same way an extremely active Emma Booth-Tucker found it: through solitude, seeking prayer, a relationship with God consistently cultivated, a daily focus on following Christ whatever the cost. Our model, of course, is Jesus (**Mark 1:35; 13:38; Matthew 26:36-42; Luke 5:16**). The Lord's Prayer itself, the model prayer He gave His disciples, even in its brevity and simplicity is a compass and guide for any one of us, whatever we face on a given day (**Matthew 6:7-15; Luke 11:1-4**).

The third way we condition ourselves for missional living is by *accepting sacrifice*. To quote Emma Booth-Tucker again: "Love without sacrifice is like a fire without a flame" (*The Officer*, 1982). Jesus is very up front about the price of living the life of a disciple in the world (**Matthew 5:10-12; 10:23; Luke 21:12; John 15:20; 6:33**). The apostle Paul reviews his missional biography and describes both joy and persecution

(II Corinthians 6:3-10), and he claims that the suffering he endures as a disciple of Jesus has no power to separate him from God's love in Christ Jesus **(Romans 8:35-39)**. As we pointed out earlier in this book, the word compassion literally means suffering with someone. It is not love as some kind of virtue, nor is it what we mean by expressing sympathy for someone who is suffering. Neither is it the suffering we endure that has nothing to do with our witness—suffering that can come to any person, which will nevertheless elicit the compassion of our Lord and other caring people. It is also not the suffering we bring upon ourselves because of our own sin or foolishness. Compassion is a suffering love directed not toward ourselves but toward another person or a people. It is Jesus on the cross, taking on the suffering and sin of the world, the culmination of a journey marked every day by acts of compassion. And it is therefore the life of Jesus' true disciples imitating their Lord.

Living missionally is not seeking suffering, but anyone who follows Jesus will inevitably come up against resistance and opposition because the lifestyle of Jesus simply does not fit the attitudes and practices of the current world order. Acts of compassion are out of place where unrepressed individualism, greedy grasping, and suspicion and hatred toward people not like us are the order of the day. Jesus' disciples will suffer because they follow a Lord who risked His life every day for the world He loved. What makes us His disciples is that we obey when He says, "Follow Me," even and especially when there is love to risk.

The fourth way we condition ourselves for missional living is *practicing on the field*. The apostle Paul admonishes the

Philippian church, first to focus their thoughts on anything that is excellent and admirable, and second to *"practice...* whatever you learned, received, heard, or saw in us" (**Philippians 4:8-9**, italics added). To an extent missional living can be taught, but if the teaching remains in the mind and is not modeled, tested, and risked on the field, it will never really be learned. Missional living is caught better than taught. Jesus' most powerful and effective transference of the values of the Kingdom of God is found in the way He models them for His disciples. Disciples are more than classroom learners; they are in particular imitators of their Rabbi-Lord. Yes, Jesus has moments of penetrating teaching, as when He preaches His radical Sermon on the Mount. But it becomes real when He demonstrates the life to which He calls us. For example, He taught us to live humbly (**Matthew 5:5; Luke 6:20**), but He actually lived and modeled it by identifying Himself with the poor (**Matthew 11:5; Luke 4:18; 7:22**) and the homeless (**Matthew 8:20; Luke 9:58**), and supremely in the self-humbling of the Incarnation and the Cross (**Philippians 2:5-8**). He is very conscious of modeling Kingdom life for His disciples, and He is especially wise in sending them out to practice the mission He has modeled for them (**Matthew 10:1-16; Mark 6:7-13; Luke 9:1-6; 10:1-3**). He admits He is taking a risk by sending them out on the field: "Look, I'm sending you as sheep among wolves." But it is on the field where they will learn practical wisdom and maintain purity under fire: "Be wise as snakes and as innocent as doves."

Malcolm Gladwell wrote a book called *Outliers* in which he studied, not only why certain people succeeded in a particular field, but especially why some became extraordinary (outliers, because they stood out from all the rest). To begin with, a certain equality of innate ability and capacity to develop is assumed with respect to those in any field he studied. The conclusion of his detailed study was that what distinguished the outliers from others in their field was time spent in the practice of their craft or calling. If the person was a basketball player, a hockey player, a violinist, a pilot—or whatever—they would stand out as extraordinary if they accumulated an enormous quantity of focused practice. By practice Gladwell means the combination of both practice in the usual sense of getting ready for actual performance *and* the performances themselves—for example, with musical groups, both practice sessions and actual concerts.

When it comes to missional living, the practice and the performance are the same. We can only learn missional living by living missionally, just as we can learn discipleship only by being disciples. This is not to say there is no real value in discipleship classes; there is. The basketball player can learn important things about playing basketball by what his coach tells him. The words of Jesus and of Paul, Peter, and other New Testament writers are crucial to our discipleship. We would be lost without them. When it comes to *living* them, however, we must start living them *now*, as best we can, trusting and relying on His guiding Spirit and imitating the Jesus we find in our spiritual mentors (**I Corinthians 4:16-17; I Thessalonians 1:5-7; Hebrews 13:7**). We test ourselves on the field. We risk falling on our faces, which we will inevitably do from time to time. We learn from these failures, as well as our successes, and our spiritual mentors help us do the learning. We are indeed practicing, but we are dead serious about it. The more we do it the more we learn, the better we get at it the more natural it becomes—and the more we are at peace with ourselves as disciples of Jesus in the world.

Jesus stands at our corps' door as we depart, and He gives each of us the same assurance He gave His disciples soon before His own departure: "My peace I give you. I give to you not as the world gives. Don't be troubles or afraid" (**John 14:27**). Perhaps we could say that the fifth way we condition ourselves to live missionally is to practice *being at peace*. As the apostle Paul assures us, we live as missional people in the guaranteed nearness of God. We live in the world with glad hearts and gentle attitudes towards others. Free of anxiety, "we bring up all of [our] requests to God in...prayers and petitions...Then the peace of God that exceeds all understanding will keep [our] hearts and minds safe in Christ Jesus" (**Philippians 4:4-7**). The peace of Christ is not an escape from the world; it is being Christ in the world.

Depend on your support system

Living missionally is not something we do alone. Disciples of Jesus are not lone individuals confronting the world for Jesus. They are soldiers in the plural. They are part of a body of Christ, whether a corps or a mission team, that worships and prays together, where members support one another and hold each other accountable for growing in holiness and living missionally. They are sent out by this body of Christ as Paul and Barnabas were sent out by the church at Antioch (**Acts 13:1-3**). As they are sent out by the body of believers, they also return for support, as Paul and Barnabas returned to their sending church, gathering the saints together, giving a full report, and then staying with the church to process this radical, new departure in mission (**14:26-28**). Undoubtedly

Paul and Barnabas then continued the mission through corre-
spondence with churches they had founded and strategized
on the next missional journey. In the meantime, they also took
the time to prepare themselves to face the church leaders in
Jerusalem to defend their conviction that Gentiles who come
to faith in Jesus were not bound by Jewish laws and customs
(*chapter 15*). None of this was done without the participation,
deliberation, support, and prayers of others.

Why do we need our Christian support system? Are we
not accountable to God as separate individuals? Let's consider three key reasons. The first is that we are all called to
imitate God, a plurality of Three Persons in One. The second
is that we are all saints in the plural. And third, we can live
missionally only in the plural.

The first reason we need our Christian support system is
that *we are imitators of God in the plural.* As those who are
called to "imitate God like dearly loved children" (**Ephesians
5:1**), we discover that our one God is a dynamic, living, loving
community of Three Persons: Father, Son, and Holy Spirit. God
is God only as all three Persons. He is a community in Himself.
As those created in His image, we are also a community; we
are only human if and when we are in community with each
other. There is nothing more inhuman than a totally alone
person who connects with no other person or who relates to
others only to exploit them for his or her own purposes. "Then
the Lord God said, 'It's not good that the human is alone'"
(**Genesis 2:18a**).

When the apostle Paul encourages the Ephesian church
to "live as people worthy of the call you received from God,"

he explains in more detail what he means by this calling (**Ephesians 4:1-6**). He speaks of being humble, patient, and gentle with each other. He says to accept each other with love, make an effort to preserve their unity and live together in a peace that ties them all together. He reminds them they "are one body and one spirit, just as God also called [them] in one hope." Together they have "one Lord, one faith, one baptism, and one God and Father of all, who is over all, through all, and in all." When you read this marvelously revealing passage, you discover that this unity in love is the shared work of Father (*v. 6*), Son (*v. 5*), and Holy Spirit (*v. 3*). The One God who is a threefold community creates us in His image as a community reflecting His very nature as a holy community united in love and purpose.

This unity in diversity is the key to our holy human-ness. We are holy in our relationships with each other and with our holy God. This must mean that a corps is fulfilling its purpose only if it is united in this way, only as its members are allowing the prayer of Jesus for His church to be fulfilled both in their life together and in their life in the world:

> I pray they will be one, Father, just as You are in Me and I am in You. I pray that they will also be in us, so that the world will believe that You sent me.... I'm in them and You are in Me so that they will be made perfectly one. Then the world will know that You sent Me and that You have loved them just as you loved Me. (*John 17:21, 23*)

Our love for the world must begin with our love for each other. A disunited corps cannot bear the fruit of the mission to which they are called. The corps' unity alone, however, doesn't necessarily mean unity in mission as well. A united corps can be united in its obsessive self-concern. Jesus calls us to unity both in the life of our corps and in our mission in the world. In the Acts of the Apostles, we read of the Holy Spirit's miracle in creating a church united in both one Body (**Acts 2:42-47**) and one mission (**4:31**). The writer to the Hebrews tells the church to "keep loving each other like family," and then, as if to caution his readers never to forget where this family love is to lead, he tells them to "open up [their] homes to guests" and to "remember prisoners as if [the church] were in prison with them, and people who are mistreated as if [the church] were in their place" (**Hebrews 13:1-3**). As those who are reconciled to God and to each other, we are entrusted with the ministry of reconciliation for the world (**II Corinthians 5:14-21**). We imitate God, who in Christ loves us into His family, who sends us into the world to represent Him and His family and spread this reconciling love—with full corps family support!

The second key reason for our needing the church, our support system, is that *disciples of Jesus are saints (holy) in the plural*. The message Jesus preaches is that the Kingdom of God has come. He invites people to enter it. He teaches them how to live in it—not by strict obedience to the law, though He doesn't do away with the law. Living in the Kingdom of God, He says, means pursuing the real purpose of the law: love of God and neighbor (**Matthew 22:34-40**). Living in the Kingdom of God means living in the plural, being part of a community of disciples who are learning and practicing together, helping each other to be a holy people. The church is the community that takes this calling seriously.

"Don't stop meeting together," says the writer to the Hebrews. It puts our faith in peril. We need to "encourage each other"; we need to "motivate each other to show love and to do good works" (**Hebrews 10:24-25**). Disciples of Jesus are *formed together*, like the early church community in Jerusalem (**Acts 2:42-47**). In His prayer for the church (**John 17**) Jesus describes His followers as the people to whom He has revealed His Father's name and ownership of them (**v. 6**), where everything the Father has given Jesus is now theirs (**v. 7**), including the words of the Father and the mission of Jesus (**v. 8**), where His disciples are now to be one as He and the Father are one (**v. 11**), where they are to accept the animosity that was before directed toward Him, and to be clear that they do not belong to a fallen world but to the Father (**vv. 14, 16**), made one together by their participation with the Trinity (**vv. 20-23**). The disciple of Jesus is always a saint together with the saints.

The togetherness of the church is deeply embedded in the New Testament. One need only explore the large number of descriptive terms of members of the Body of Christ that have a certain preposition attached to the words themselves. The preposition in the original Greek is *sun*, which means "with,"or "in company with," or "together with." Used as a prefix to another word that refers to some calling in the church, it makes that calling something that is shared by others. When the combination of this prefix with a calling is used in the Greek, it is often translated in English by preceding the particular calling with the word "fellow" or "co-." So we have the church comprised of "fellow [or co-] workers" (**II Corinthians 6:1; 8:23; Philippians 2:25**), "fellow [or co-] strugglers" (**Philippians 1:27**), "fellow [or co-] slaves"

(**Colossians 1:7**), "fellow [or co-] prisoners" (**Romans 16:7; Colossians 4:10**), "fellow [or co-] soldiers" (**Philippians 2:25**), to mention only a few of the ways in the church members share in everything. In everything we are and do in the corps in the name of Jesus, all of us are partners as much as Paul and Timothy were (**II Corinthians 8:23**); we are a part of it. We are a *fellow*-ship, fellows together. Even though none of us does or participates in everything directly, we all participate by our support and prayer. And even though we may not be experiencing the individual positive successes, challenges, or trials of other soldiers in the corps, we are with them as fellows in Christ. This is how the Body of Christ works, and when this doesn't happen, the Body isn't working well. It may, in fact, be ill.

Another way of describing this plurality of our lives as fellow Christians is for us to see our own corps as a *covenant community*. You may have noticed that what used to be called *The Articles of War*, the pledge signed by those who were enrolled as soldiers, is now called *The Soldier's Covenant*. The word covenant, of course, appears in both the Old and New Testaments. In the Old Testament we meet a covenant-making God who calls Israel to enter into a covenant as His chosen people. He gives them His promise and calls them to give Him their obedience (**Exodus 19:1-6**). This covenant binds Israel together as a people, a nation, of which all Israelites are a part and in which they find their identity. The covenant assumes a covenant people.

In the New Testament, the writer to the Hebrews speaks of the church as a community bound together by Jesus in "a better covenant that is enacted with better promises"

(**Hebrews 8:6**). Whereas the Jews were drawn by their covenant to Mt. Zion, the followers of Jesus are now drawn into "a Kingdom that can't be shaken" where together they serve Jesus with gratitude (**12:22-24**). Perhaps corps would be greatly helped by seeing themselves as a covenant community, together living in gratitude for what God has given the world through Jesus, together exploring and putting into practice what it means to be a covenant community of Jesus' disciples, together supporting one another in love and service. Saints in the plural.

The third reason for needing the church, our support system, is that *we succeed in the plural.* If the corps is a covenant community, and if each group within the corps is a smaller version of this covenant community, then corps members will most likely be on the same page and corps programs will most likely work together as part of a whole. While Keitha and I were university students, Jim and Ruth Osborne became our corps officers. One of the many things that impressed us about their pastoral leadership was that they began immediately to get the whole corps on the same page. They didn't call it building a covenant community, but I'm convinced that's what it was. In retrospect, I can now understand that they were, in fact, forming such a community. The corps was there to build the Kingdom of God in people's lives and to model the Kingdom in the life and mission of the corps congregation. Sometimes corps officers are afraid to challenge and even confront soldiers about their non-covenantal laxity, fearing that doing so will drive more away from their already dwindling corps population. The Osbornes were not controlled by such fear, and the corps grew.

The most important outcome when a corps becomes a covenantal community lies outside the life of the corps itself. It lies in the ultimate purpose for which the corps exists: to be God's missional people in the world. The bands, classes, and societies of early Methodism were a marvelous expression of such covenantal communities. These intimate groups prayed for themselves, other groups, and for the world, and they held each member accountable both for their own spiritual journey and for their witness during the week. The early Salvation Army also had much of this character as a community that prayed for each other and held one another accountable. I believe that as long as a corps lives its life as this kind of covenantal community, it will prosper in ways that matter in the Kingdom of God.

We have come to the third reason we depend on our corps congregation. For the Army, as for any church, *we succeed only in the plural.* By "success" I do not mean growth by any means. Some means of church growth are superficial, or merely market oriented, or appeal to self-centered desires or escapism or fear. By "success" I mean building a community of sanctified Christians who are growing in holiness and living their whole lives for the mission of Jesus. I mean a community invested in every member and every member invested in mission.

In terms of mission some, probably most, corps consist of two groups: missionally active members and missionally inactive members—usually the larger group. They have probably come to accept this partition as normal, when from the perspective of what it means to live in the Kingdom of God—*i.e.*, be a Christian!—it is sadly abnormal. Indeed, the missionally partitioned corps may have limited success through a few missionally active members, but it is nowhere near meeting its true potential and only partially obeying the Great Commission (**Matthew 28:18-20; Mark 16:15; Luke 24:46-48**). A corps where all members (soldiers and adherents) are disciples living missionally becomes what Ken Callahan calls "a legend on the community grapevine," not just because of one or two effective corps programs that reach the community, but also, especially, because all members consider themselves to be in mission wherever they are their whole week. *This* is normal missional behavior for a corps.

Harold Hill has done an interesting study of how leadership and participation have evolved from The Salvation Army's beginnings, especially in the Western world (*Leadership In The Salvation Army: A Case Study In Clericalization*). What Hill's study reveals is that while the Army began primarily as a lay movement, over time more and more control was transferred from the non-officer soldiers into the hands of the officer class. This is exactly what George Scott-Railton feared would lead to the destruction of the Army as a dynamic and effective missional force in the world! What began as a movement of missional volunteers became an institution run primarily by organizational professionals. Put alongside this development a growing accommodation of Christians in general, including Salvationists, to the culture around them, leading to a separation between corps involvement and their very different life in their world during the week. For many corps, corps officers became the ones who do mission, along with a few interested and committed soldiers. The idea that every Salvationist is called to mission has been lost in those corps, as has the means to support and enable it.

In chapter 9 we spoke of how essential it is to engage corps members who see their attendance on Sunday mornings and for special corps events as an all-sufficient practice of their Christian faith. These dormant corps members are among our most important challenges. We do not need to make them feel guilty because they're not more active in the corps. We need to help them see their entire week as the mission field to which they've been called. We need to help them see their corps as a spiritual home that will nurture them in holy living and support them as their spiritual family. Dormancy is not death; it is life asleep that needs to be awakened. It is like putting that dry and seemingly devoid of life flower bulb into fertile soil, watering it, and over time seeing it blossom into wonder. This does not happen to a lone individual on his own. It happens to an under-developed Christian whose spiritual family helps him discover who he really is in Christ and how to start living that way 24/7. A missional Christian with a missional family.

Most of a soldier's life is not lived in or at the corps. It is lived in the world. The corps, nevertheless, is absolutely essential to his life in the world if that world is to be the mission to which he is passionately and unquestionably committed. He will be effective in that mission as one who believes Christ is already present in his world and as one who has the prayers and backing of his corps family and the guiding presence of the Holy Spirit.

Many corps have cliques. Cliques are divisive and often cruel. Because they are based on deep insecurity and operate by the un-Christlike principle of exclusion, they are really unhappy groups to be a part of. Whatever bliss is achieved in cliques is a sick cruelty. A good way forward is to replace them with corps mission teams: teams that pray for their members and for other teams, teams focused on their spiritual growth and the spiritual growth of their corps, teams in love with the world for whom Christ gave His life and who hold one another accountable for living missionally, teams who have *real* fun.

This is the kind of plurality through which our corps will find real success. A corps must stay united and together so that members can succeed apart. To give a faithful witness in the world is why we condition ourselves as disciples and why we are part of a corps congregation that supports us and that we support. Jesus calls us out, and He calls us in—in to join together in worship, prayer, and love; in to reconnect with the holy Body of Christ; in to be accountable and affirmed as God's missional people.

Give your witness

To live missionally is to respond to our calling to give witness in the world. Taking their cue from God's covenant with Abraham, Lynette Edge and Gregory Morgan point out that we can view that calling as a *calling to bless* (*Partnering with God: Being a Missional Salvationist*, pp. 21ff.). As Abraham was called to make a great nation that would be a blessing to "all the families of the earth" (**Genesis 12:1-3**), so the apostle Paul takes this calling of Abraham and claims that it was "the Gospel in advance" through which "all the Gentiles will be blessed" (**Galatians 3:8**). We do not give witness by disengaging from the world and turning our backs on those God has called us to bless in Christ. We give witness by being a blessing, by sharing Christly compassion, by offering hope.

To do this we must seek to live Jesus, plant Jesus, and risk doing so behind enemy lines.

First, we give witness by *living Jesus*. What does this mean? How can we possibly measure up to the life of Jesus? We can't. What we can do is ask the Holy Spirit, the Spirit of Jesus, to purify and empower us to have sufficient resemblance. As Jesus taught us the values of the Kingdom of God, so we can seek to live by them (**Matthew, chapters 5-7**). As Jesus "traveled around doing good" (**Acts 10:38a**), so we can seek to bless others and do them good as Jesus did (**Luke 6:35**). As Jesus "traveled around...healing everyone oppressed by the devil" (**Acts 10:38b**), so we can bring healing to the sick and hurting in His name (**Luke 9:2; Acts 3:6-8; 14:8-10; 28:8; James 5:16**). We live Jesus by adopting His mindset and sharing His compassion with others.

We are called to live Jesus all the time. We do it humbly with full recognition of our meagerness and with full confidence that Christ can make Himself known even through that meagerness. This realization must surely help us understand the apostle Paul's rather surprising statement to the Philippian church that though "some preach Christ with jealous and competitive motives," he is glad simply because "Christ is proclaimed [made known] in every possible way" (**Philippians 1:15-18**). Paul certainly had strong disagreements and even condemnation over the theology and/or lifestyle of certain church members or leaders. But here, following Jesus (**Matthew 7:1; Luke 6:37; John 8:15; 12:47**), he seems to be at peace that in spite of the mixed motives of some and the meagerness of the witness of all Christians, Christ is made known, openings are made, the word is getting out.

The message for all of Christ's followers is this: Be at peace. Neither you nor any other Christian is perfect. Live Jesus as best you can, all the time. Confess your inadequacy, let fellow Christians teach and mentor you, and keep getting better at living Jesus. Always look for Jesus wherever you are, imagine what He's up to, be His co-partner—and people who don't see Jesus as you can might very well see some Jesus in you.

The second way we give witness is by *planting Jesus*. As we have seen, our witness is first to imitate Jesus in the world, to be icons of Christ. It is also to find fertile ground and plant the seeds of God's Kingdom, to begin to make disciples. Jesus frequently likens our witness in the world to planting seeds. In the Parable of the Sower, He seems to be advising His disciples to seek good soil for planting, to disciple where good conditions both for seeds sprouting and for sustained growth exist. Conversion without discipling is a misfire (**Matthew 13:1-9, 18-23; Mark 4:3-9, 13-20; Luke 8:4-8, 11-15**).

Evangelism is not a contrivance. It is as natural as wisely planting seeds. In the natural world God created, living things multiply either by cell division or by seed implantation. Disciples of Jesus are of the species called humankind. They use cell division when a Christian group decides to divide to start an additional group, and they practice seed implantation when a disciple invests himself in bringing someone to faith and continued discipling. This, by the way, is how the New Testament church grew, and how every Christian movement has grown, including the early Salvation Army.

Planting the seeds of the Gospel can be a risky business, as Jesus has said. It depends on where we do the sowing.

Sowing seeds in our own backyard with family and friends is a good place to start, though interestingly, in some ways, here the sowing is more difficult, even threatening. These are the people who know us best and from whom it is most difficult to hide our imperfections: We are exposed. Here evangelical courage requires plenty of humility! Sowing Gospel seeds elsewhere means building relationships in other spaces we inhabit in a way that gives us opportunities to demonstrate the attitudes and values of the Kingdom of God. Here the challenge is not so much that we are known too well as that we need to be known better. Here, in all humility, we need to expose the depth of our commitment to Jesus and His way of life. It will soon become apparent that we live by values that clash with many of the commonly accepted values of those we meet and those with whom we associate. We find ourselves in a minority; we may even be ostracized. We are in a position of weakness.

Jesus teaches us that when our holy love for others and our faithfulness to Kingdom values puts us in such seemingly weak positions, the outcome is redemptive. His own life is the proof: It was only because He loved us so deeply, even to the extent of refusing to defend His own life, that He freed the human race to "to want and actually to live out [God's] good purposes" (**Philippians 2:6-13**). Paul claimed that when he was in a weak position, then he was strong (**II Corinthians 12:10**). Being willing to be made weak for love of others as Jesus did puts us in an ironic position of strength. "By turning the other cheek," says Harry Dean, "offering the cloak as well, and going the second mile we wrest the initiative from the antagonist and assume moral command of the situation" (*Power and Glory*). Simon Tugwell uses the analogy of a good judo expert who uses the strength of his opponent to bring him to the ground (*Prayer*). The irony of God: What we call power, He calls impotence. We see humbling ourselves as weakness or defeat; He sees it as reliance on the power of the Spirit, the only power that endures, the only form of courage that ultimately wins. And that is why "the weakness of God is stronger than human strength" (**I Corinthians 1:25b**). To live Jesus is to risk the strength of this weakness, and to plant Jesus is to draw others to such a life of humbling, without which the love Jesus taught and lived is not possible.

The third way we give witness is to *give our lives behind enemy* lines. Our job as disciples is to plant Christ *wherever we are*. Along similar lines, Phil Wall proposes adopting a missional battle plan different than the one we typically use. The plan is to "get behind enemy lines." Wall uses an analogy drawn from a radical change in military strategy proposed by a British military expert, Col. Sir Archibald David Sterling. During the First World War, Sterling saw that the strategy of charging across the battlefield in large numbers was "no longer fit for purpose in the age of the Gatling gun." Thousands were mowed down as they went over the top of the trenches. Sterling went on "to invent the SAS whose focus was to get behind enemy lines and undermine their capacity to fight by blowing up... infrastructure, planes, bridges, etc." (www.infinitumlife.com). Wall is suggesting that frontal assaults as a missional strategy are also not effective in most cases, especially in a world where people aren't as predisposed to the church as they once were. Furthermore, it is a strategy that relies too much on mere cleverness and strength. In our day we are especially called to be scattered throughout the world, convincing the unbelieving by our authentic living and holy Christlikeness, not the impressiveness of our frontal assaults. Our calling is to infiltrate and infect the world with Jesus.

The enemy, of course, is not people. "We aren't fighting against human enemies but against rulers, authorities, forces of cosmic darkness, and spiritual powers of evil in the heavens" (**Ephesians 6:12**). Our armor is therefore spiritual: "the full armor of God" (**v. 13**). Our power comes from God Himself and is "at work in Christ" and is now "working among us believers." It is a power far above these powers "and any power that might be named not only now but in the future" (**1:18-23**). The church is God's instrument to show these powers "the many different varieties of His wisdom" (**3:10**). These powers were actually created by God through Christ and for Christ (**Colossians 1:16**), but they, like the human race, are in rebellion. What is clear for the apostle Paul, however, is that Christ is still "the head of every ruler and authority" (**2:10**); in fact, He has "disarmed" or freed us of them (**v. 15**). Yes, we still have to take these now insidious, corrupt powers seriously, but we do so with the assurance that their defeat and ultimate submission is real. Our calling is to confront them and teach them their validity is gone and their days are numbered (**Romans 8:38-39**).

It is true, as we've seen, that these powers can and often do invade and corrupt the church itself. We certainly must, therefore, confront them at home base: Our mission begins in domestic territory. The corps itself needs to have credible resemblance to the Kingdom of God. An important part of achieving that resemblance is to nurture active compassion for the world, and this compassion will draw corps members away from internal bickering and cliquing and out into the world mission field. This outward focus will have a purifying effect on corps members.

I recall a beautiful piece by Samuel Moor Shoemaker titled "I Stand by the Door." It is an eloquent appeal by a respected Christian leader pleading with his fellow Christians not to abandon the door between the church and the world. Yes, he says, explore the spiritual depths of your new home, grow in grace, and enjoy the fellowship of your Christian brothers and sisters. But don't forget to stand by that door of separation to touch the "blind, groping hands... [of] starving beggars" and welcome them into the place of saving grace, the home for which they have been longing ("I Stand by the Door," quoted in *A Guide to Prayer*, pp. 305-397).

Shoemaker wrote his piece over 50 years ago when truly welcoming and caring churches attracted seekers. Today we hope every corps is such a place, a place where anyone is welcome and made to feel a part of an inclusively loving congregation. The fact is, however, that being a warm, welcoming congregation, as essential as it is, is not alone sufficient for our day. The corps' door must not only be wide open for new people to come in, it must also be wide open for church members to be sent out, each on his or her own mission for the rest of the week. Jesus stands at that door, inviting us to live Him and plant Him wherever we are, and especially behind enemy lines. Only then will the church begin, over time, to reach the whole world. By the way, this is what our early Salvation Army was so good at doing. Without earthly power or support, they allowed the love of God to humble them and gift them with courage. And where we are successful at it today, we are truly building the Kingdom of God in a way that makes a lasting difference—a transforming blessing behind enemy lines!

FOR REFLECTION & PRAYER

Which Scripture verse or passage in the chapter spoke most deeply to you, or challenged you most? Say why.

Condition yourself

Personal: What is the relationship between solitude/prayer and mission in your own life currently?

Is there a step you can take to integrate them and thereby make both of them better as far as your own life with Christ is concerned? Please describe the step.

As you look at the levels of clutter and complexity in your life, is there a step you can take to help you focus on and live better your calling as a disciple? Please describe the step.

We all make sacrifices for certain purposes or outcomes. Is there some sacrifice you are making for a purpose that you now suspect is not worth it in light of your calling as Jesus' disciple? And is there a new purpose you now feel will be worth making a sacrifice for? Please describe.

How is your conditioning for discipleship coming along? Are you using actual mission(s) you are undertaking as learning experiences? If so, who are you using to help you debrief and learn? For example, a mentor or a mission team. Please describe. If you are not using your mission involvement also as a learning experience, what step could you take to do so?

Your corps: Can you think of a step your corps can take to help you and other Salvationists condition themselves for missional living?

Depend on your support system

Personal: What in your corps is the means or medium by which you derive the most personal support?

Please describe why.

What does it mean to you personally that you are not called to be a lone saint but a saint among a family of saints?

How specifically does your corps and fellow Salvationists help you in your pursuit of holiness?

Do you think that you contribute to the unity of your corps? If so, how does this contribution help to bring your corps together?

Can you describe an experience where you personally saw your corps succeed in the plural? What contribution did you make to that success?

Your corps: How can your corps become a better and more effective covenant community, united together in Christ in its purpose, life, and mission? Be specific.

What could you personally do to help in this process? Be specific.

Give your witness

Personal: How seriously do you take your calling to be a blessing to others?

Is there any specific way you can improve your response to this calling?

In what way could you improve your reflection of Jesus in the specific settings of your own life?

Consider the places and occasions of your own week. Where specifically could you start fresh to plant Jesus (begin to disciple in or toward Jesus)?

Your corps: How united and effective is your corps in supporting the mission of members "behind the lines" during the week?

What could you do specifically to move your corps toward becoming a helpful missional support family? Is there someone in the corps you could talk to about this?

CHAPTER 12

GROW LIKE A MOVEMENT

*[Many denominations] seek salvation in maintaining
each its own traditional and past historical structure,
rather than in openness and readiness for changes and
new elements added to the whole structure... The
Church is not a dead, unapproachable, mighty or rich
body, but is Christ's living and growing body... [It] always
grows intensively and extensively. Her members have the
same faith and hope for "those far and those near"
(Ephesians 2:13, 17, 19). (Markus Barth, The Broken
Wall, pp. 118, 120)*

*As biblical believers, we do not believe that you have
to follow forms derived from completely different
cultures and situations. We are free to follow Jesus in
ways that are genuinely meaningful for the culture we
live in. We can and must adapt to the ever-changing
conditions in which we find ourselves. We cannot make
cultural expressions sacred and inviolable—doing so
ends in a dangerous idolatry. The church must not
become the object of its own affection. The church
ought to represent a dynamic cultural expression of the
people of God in anygiven place.*
(Alan Hirsch, The Forgotten Ways, p. 155)

Movements want to transform the world. The movement
that became known as The Salvation Army wanted to trans-

form the world by engaging the people who knew least about the Christian faith and introducing them to Jesus. The failure of most churches to take converts from there brought the introduced and converted back to the movement. The movement (Army) then set out to mold soldier-disciples of these new recruits. It grew not by adding new members but by training and commissioning eager soul fighters.

Inevitably, over time movements take on some of the characteristics of an institution. The greater the institutionalization, the greater the focus on the prosperity and survival of the institution itself, and the greater the illusion that the institution itself is the key to the success of the original mission. Some institutions exist primarily or even totally for its members. Others exist for both its members and for non-members it serves. I consider the current Salvation Army—in the Western world especially—to be one of the latter. Known for our compassionate service to those who in one way or another are marginalized, we receive generous support from the public to carry out those services. The movement impulse is still there; compassion still flows through our veins.

There are forces, however, that threaten to constrict the arteries and block the flow. I'm convinced we can trace the problem back to four factors. One is the increasing demand made upon fewer and fewer of our soldiers to carry the weight of our mission. This unfortunate division of labor is supported by corps taking on more and more the character of an institution. In the institutional corps division of labor is the rule and mission is now falsely seen as the responsibility of the missionally gifted and the hired professionals. The result is that in an increasing number of corps the mission is carried by the corps officers, paid employees, and a very few or no soldiers. The majority of soldiers remain missionally passive.

This missional passivity is further supported by the second factor: As our social outreach has expanded, we have had to hire more employees to implement and administer it—so much so that in most places these employees far outnumber our officers. It may well be that in some commands the majority of them are not Salvationists, which itself sometimes creates a disconnect between the movement's primary mission and its social outreach. It may well be that the great majority of them see no relation between making disciples of Jesus and the services they are rendering.

The third factor contributes even further to the missional blockage: As Salvationists become separated from social outreach and as some corps become more like self-centered institutions, corps programs that were originally very effective means of including, converting, and discipling new people may evolve into programs primarily for Salvationists.

The fourth factor relates specifically to our movement's original purpose once it became a church home to its converts. That purpose is to make radical followers of Jesus (*i.e.*, disciples)—or to use our Army terminology, "Blood and Fire soldiers." Groups that were originally formed to convert sinners and grow disciples sometimes, perhaps often, lose this purpose and become programs. They may even become ends in themselves—*i.e.*, required to be done by headquarters though often missionally ineffective. The idea that the ultimate goal of *everything* we do is to make disciples who then *themselves* become the compassionate extension of Jesus in the world may be lost in the frenetic executions of our programed gatherings.

I believe the truth is this: Our Army in the Western world will continue to decline spiritually and numerically if we do not make disciples our priority. I am not at all suggesting that we somehow start pulling back on our social services. On the contrary, I'm proposing we begin implementing what is already taking place in some corps: Salvationists being discipled, Salvationists discipling others, Salvationists sharing the compassion of Christ with others, especially the marginalized and sometimes in appropriate ways with those the Army serves through its formal social services.

This is not a strategy that can be programmatically detailed from headquarters. It can only be homegrown on the field with full accountability *to* headquarters, and encouragement and resourcing *from* headquarters. It is not a wholesale declaration from headquarters that every corps must take this step. Lord knows many corps are not ready or inclined to do so. If a corps is not seriously making disciples who know they are called to live as disciples 24/7, to disciple others, and to share the compassion of Christ with others, that corps is not ready to embark on mission in new ways. The way forward is led by those few corps who will lead our Army back to where we started, and perhaps "to know the place for the first time," to use T.S. Eliot's phrase.

I believe it is possible that a corps that has lost its missional impulse can regain it if some soldiers and adherents get serious—in heart, mind, and action—about disciple living. Not a narrow, cozy, holier-than-thou kind of discipleship, but an imitate Jesus, compassionate, open to the world discipleship—real holiness. Such Salvationists can form a critical mass of missional disciples who form a cell of mutual support, accountable to each other and the corps officer, prayer, and missional planning. They may commit to an existing corps program as the most promising group through which to make disciples who disciple, reach and disciple new people, and serve the marginalized. Or they may initiate a new mission in the community, with encouragement from corps officers and headquarters who are able to transcend a touch of nervousness over the risk of a new departure. I am fully aware of liability issues which must be considered. All the more reason for open lines of communication and clear accountability!

Such new initiatives require a dose of courage and awareness of possible failure. Headquarters might want to encourage missional initiatives that could succeed but also fail. Ken Callahan suggests giving "The Most Excellent Failure" award to the corps whose new venture did not pay off but was a valuable means of missional learning.

If a corps is ready to embark on this venture to discover where and how this Army started and was so effective missionally, and to discover new ways this can happen today, I suggest there are four areas where we must succeed. We must:

i. Make, develop, and keep making disciples

ii. Learn how to grow organically

iii. Learn how to grow the mission

iv. Be willing to colonize

Make, develop, and keep making disciples

As I have emphasized throughout this book, a disciple of Jesus is not someone who has been converted and joined a church and now lives contentedly in the permanent and guaranteed benefit of his status in grace. Neither is he someone who, because he has claimed a second blessing of sanctification, feels he has no further need of spiritual progress. A disciple of Jesus is always seeking to "be growing in the knowledge of God" (**Colossians 1:10c**), to "grow in every way into Christ" (**Ephesians 4:15b**), and to "imitate God...[by] following the example of Jesus" (**Ephesians 5:1-2**). The goal of discipling, according to Paul, is "love from a pure heart, a good conscience, and a sincere faith" (**I Timothy 1:5**). This growth never ceases. We know from biology that an organism that stops growing is an organism that is dying. That principle applies to disciples, as well.

A corps needs to look seriously at how well it is forming disciples. Discipling does not happen on its own, just as any life form can stay alive and grow only if it is both being fed and feeding itself. A corps must provide spiritual nurture by every possible means including mentoring, modeling, preaching, teaching, Bible study, using discipling resources, *etc.* Each Salvationist must be encouraged and helped to take proactive responsibility for his own formation as a disciple, for which he is accountable to another disciple. Infants rely heavily on others for nurture, but as they mature they must also learn to find the particular spiritual sustenance they need. Disciple formation requires both a faith community that nurtures its members and a willingness on the part of the disciple to initiate and carry through his own formation as Christ's follower.

Getting more people into our corps building or center is not the final outcome our Lord seeks. If we think it is, we are paving our way to spiritual death. A corps starts dying when it thinks it is the point of arrival, the end product. Christianity is dying in the Western world because most Western churches think that once they get people into their church, missional success has been accomplished. All that has been accomplished is that we have gotten more people into the church—but not necessarily gotten more people in than have left!

A corps is not called to grow *per se*. It is called to make disciples, which is the Great Commission of Jesus (**Matthew 28:18-20**). This is our mission, pure and simple. We are not called to make more members for our corps. We are called to make disciples and to populate our corps with disciples who are being discipled and are discipling others. If we are not growing with disciples, we are building a house of cards.

Our growth as a movement of disciples will indeed happen when: 1. Our mission to make disciples remains primary, and 2. Our (institutionalized) corps retains the mentality, passion, and focus of a movement. This means the corps must center everything on Jesus, growing as His disciples, and keeping His calling ever as our guide and challenge. It also means getting over our fear of failure when considering a new missional venture. The worst that can happen is a failure we can learn from!

The prophecy of **Psalm 22:25-31** that all the earth will come back to the Lord will be realized only if His church will get unsettled and become the discipling force its members are called to be. How will this happen? We can take our cue from

Jesus whose descriptions of Kingdom of God growth reveal a strong predilection for organic metaphors. The apostle Paul's metaphor for the church as a human body is the furthest thing from institutional. What if our understanding of the church in the modern age, which emerged from the highly organized mechanical age, has lost much of its New Testament character as a living, throbbing, growing organism that resembles the living Christ?

There is no such thing as a one- or two-dimensional organism. The church doesn't exist on paper. It lives and grows in three dimensions or it dies. The first dimension is each person's spiritual growth: disciples are being formed. The second is Body of Christ growth: the congregation is being formed together. The third is missional growth: the congregation is opening its doors to and for the world. These three dimensions are not a sequence. All three work together at the same times because all three dimensions are essential for the life of a disciple of Jesus. A disciple does not graduate from mastering his personal growth before he is ready for full participation in the spiritual growth of his congregation (corps). Nor does he wait till he has become a good congregational (corps) member before he allows himself to be launched into the mission field. As soon as he becomes Jesus' disciple, he is growing himself, participating in the growing spiritual life of his church home (corps), and practicing his Christian faith in the world.

Learn how to grow organically

A corps (literally, a "body") is our expression of the Body of Christ. As we well know, some corps have little resemblance to a Body of Christ, and some corps have either a few or many occasions when they resemble a Body of Christ. No corps always resembles a Body of Christ—which is not surprising when we consider some of the problems and failures of churches described in the New Testament letters. No corps is perfect spiritually, and even those corps that stand out as best resembling the Body of Christ must keep themselves humbled lest by comparing themselves to other corps they acquire a pride destructive of the spirit of Jesus. If the corps is not growing in holiness, it is in spiritual decline. No corps is in stasis!

One of the growth metaphors used by Jesus that best addresses the spiritual growth of a corps is Jesus comparing Himself to a vine and we as His disciples, the branches (**John 15:1-8**). All branches of a plant must grow, or they die. Sometimes they must be trimmed in order to keep the branch healthy and fruit bearing. In fact, trimming is one of the most important and potentially positive actions a corps must be willing to undertake for the sake of both its disciple growth and its mission. Above all, a corps must maintain a dependent connection to the vine itself. If that nurturing connection is compromised, the branch dies.

Sometimes a corps has become so disconnected from Jesus that it is dead. The only way to restore life is to start all over. Other corps may not be dead, but there are forces and influences that prevent the needed spiritual growth. Those forces and influences must be dealt with in love, but firmly. Otherwise, spiritual growth will be hampered and health will decline. Those corps we can describe as healthy branches of the true vine must be diligent to nurture growth and never to be content with their state; they continue to grow or they decline.

Paul's metaphor of the church as the Body of Christ teaches us that the Body must absolutely stay connected to the Head (Christ), who "nourishes and supports the whole body through the joints and ligaments, so that the body grows with *a growth that is from God"* (**Colossians 2:19**, italics added). This means that Christ is the one we must allow to be the inspiration and originator of all decisions and actions of our corps, and that those decisions and actions must specifically reflect the life and mission to which Christ calls us, His disciples, according to Scripture.

Learn how to grow the mission

In this and the following section, I am especially indebted to missiologist Alan Hirsch's teaching and writing for helping me both to see the New Testament church's mission in a new light and to understand some of the key ways it relates to the cultures and communities we are called to reach today. Mission isn't just a task; it is first of all and most essentially a response to God's gracious love for us and for the whole world. *Missioners are who we are in Christ!* We Christians are all called to the mission of multiplying ourselves. To use another organic metaphor, we are like starfish. Break a piece off that starfish, and that piece may well grow into another starfish. Mission is leaving pieces of ourselves in the world every day, maybe in some act of compassion, of help, of witness: and that piece, over time and given the right conditions, may grow someone into a disciple. "Go and make disciples," says Jesus to all of us.

As the church is a living organism and not a machine, the growth of its mission takes place in an organic rather than a mechanical way. Mission is not so much calculated or imposed as it is a natural process in the life of the corps family, like the way plants and animals reproduce. When a movement like The Salvation Army evolves into an institution, things which were done spontaneously and naturally tend to be preserved as they were, becoming things done automatically and mechanically. Repetition of the exact same initiatives and programs becomes the organizational *modus operandi* and are measured by statistical reports. Doing the same things with a change of window dressing and hoping for different results, however, only continues the stagnation. If, on the other hand, we began to see our mission as an ever-changing organic process, it would begin to prosper.

To help us see this, let's begin with the world God created. What can it teach us about mission growth? It is interesting that our eleven Articles of Doctrine have no doctrine of Creation. They do mention that God is "the Creator, Preserver, and Governor of all things," but they tell us nothing about His Creation and our specific place in it and responsibility for it. God has put into place very specific ways organic forms perpetuate their species:

- Organically, not mechanically: All life forms (including humans) grow exponentially.

- Interrelatedly, not independently: All organic growth (including among humans) takes place through relationships within the species.

- By fertilization, not cloning: This is true of almost all animal species, including humans. Human cloning, like all cloning, can only produce an exactly same human—*i.e.*, over time a human that cannot adapt to new threats in the environment for which fertilization by another human with some differences in genetic code could provide that protection or ability to adapt. Why would God want us to grow disciples in a way that bears no similarity to the ways every other species in the planet perpetuates itself?

Consider how multi-celled forms of life reproduce. The cell of one plant is fertilized by the cell of another plant of the same species, thus helping ensure that any genetic weakness in one will less likely be carried to the new plant. With animals that are divided by gender, the same principle applies. We will leave the reproducing by cell division of one-cell animals to the next section on colonizing.

It was inevitable that our movement would become an institution. Unfortunately, a part of that process was the pressure to normalize discipleship: to make clones who are like us and who conform to the same institutional norms. Discipling, however, is not cloning. Clones are ineffective in a changing world. Yes, there are certainly specifics of discipleship that remain consistent from age to age. All disciples are called to live holy lives according to Jesus' teaching and example. They are called to imitate Jesus and have His mind. They are called to pursue the power of love and renounce the love of power. In a rapidly changing world, however, they are also called to courage and creativity in mission. Many of the same plans and programs for reaching people effectively may not work now or in a different situation or culture. Cross-fertilization is necessary. We must reproduce disciples who can meet the new challenges of making disciples of all cultures, age groups, ethnicities, and races—and especially the marginalized.

One unfortunate expression of the cloning tendency is for a corps to place the priority on growing by addition. Growth by addition is very mechanical; it is the numbers game. We set goals like increasing the number of new soldiers by five this year or increasing Sunday school attendance by 10 percent. This can actually be done by meaningless enrollments or by gimmicks. Because what is important are the numbers, it may or may not result in making real disciples, and more likely will not. Numbers also suggest more of the same. In fact, in this age of mass production we tend to think of growth as acquiring more and more of the same product. When we buy a product we count on it being a replica as reliable as another copy of that same product. If the product is the same, all we need to do is count. Numbers do not measure the real potential for discipleship in the unique individuals who come within our influence.

Our Army does not need soldiers like us. It needs soldiers not like us, disciples who bring unique perspectives, understandings, and capacities to relate to the changing needs and cultures around us. It needs soldiers who can invade foreign territories as our Army forebears did. If we pursue the numbers game, we will continue to decline as we have been in the Western world for decades and our mission to make disciples will become increasingly irrelevant. Those who live by goals of addition must also live by the inevitable reality of subtraction. Planning by addition cannot fulfill the Great Commission.

The happy alternative is to allow our mission to thrive by multiplication. Multiplication is a strategy for discipling and missional growth that is based on the premise that every disciple is a discipler and missional growth is therefore exponential as growth is in the natural world. If every disciple disciples, then counting becomes almost impossible. How does an organization like The Salvation Army keep track if every Salvationist is discipling people in their own sphere of life, especially when their discipling is at different stages with the people they are influencing for Christ? And what if those persons a Salvationist is discipling come together to form a group, a kind of mini-corps, an outpost of their own. How do we work the numbers? Exponential growth doesn't calculate very easily, but it's the only growth that will reach the world for Christ. Our Army must decide if it will measure success by numbers or by people discipled.

Be willing to colonize

The phenomenal growth of the church in Acts happens, it seems, in exponential surges of disciples witnessing (**Acts 1:13; 2:41, 47; 4:4; 5:14; 21:20**), and "God [making] it grow" (**I Corinthians 3:6b**). Indeed, the Gospel seems to have a life of its own. Paul talks about the Gospel itself expanding within the borders and beyond (**II Corinthians 10:13-16**). In his letter to the Colossian church, he uses an organic metaphor in describing the Gospel "bearing fruit and growing among you [the Colossian church] since the day you heard and truly understood God's grace, in the same way that it is bearing fruit and growing in the whole world" (**Colossians 1:6-8**). He seems to be referring to both spiritual and numerical growth, suggesting that if we truly grow spiritually, we will grow numerically. A true Christian spirituality blossoms in growth.

Here is where we draw on another organic analogy. One-celled animals and viruses have an interesting way of reproducing by cell division and multiplication. One cell divides to produce two one-celled life forms, they then produce four, and within a relatively short period of time, the one has become a multitude, a colony, if you like. To kill a disease caused by one-cell life forms, we would have to stop this highly efficient means of reproduction. Rapid exponential growth of this kind is hard to contain, as we discover when a particularly virulent strain of the germ or virus is the culprit.

What if Salvationists took this model of organic growth and imitated it in their approach to mission on the broader scale? What if a corps went viral! What if they grew mission by cell division! What if a small group of missional Salvationists in the corps—we'll call the group a cell—doubled its original size and decided to divide in two, each of the two cells then growing and, as per the plan, dividing in two again, until over time the corps looked like a colony of Christ? This, in fact, is how the early church grew in the cities of the Roman Empire: The mother church (which over time became the cathedral church) seeded within the environs new cells that became new congregations with disciples sent from its growing congregation. Try to imagine what it would look like for a corps to do something similar!

Or, what if a corps took the model of Booth's city, farm, and overseas colonies (The Darkest England Scheme) and applied it to each Salvationist in the corps by training him or her to be a Christ colonizer by spreading the DNA of Christ, bringing the values of the Kingdom of God to bear in every part of their lives and associations—colonize not through power but through love, advocacy, empowerment, witness? What if the whole corps went viral?

Keep in mind that by colonizing the Gospel in this way, disciples of Jesus are not trying to take over foreign land; they are reclaiming what Christ has already won. The whole world has been reconciled to God in Christ (**II Corinthians 5:19; Colossians 1:19-20**). Christ preached peace to those both far and near (**Ephesians 2:17**). Christ not only fills His church, He ascended to Heaven so that He might fill everything (**Ephesians 1:23b; 4:10**). Therefore, the church cannot exist without making Christ (the Head) known to those still far (**Ephesians 3:10-12; 6:15**). The church is the sign and seal of God's claim upon the world. One of the Army's mottos that has stayed with us almost from the beginning of the movement is "ALL THE WORLD"!

Perhaps we could think of our missional colonizing by remembering our Methodist roots. We previously mentioned that Methodism was primarily successful in mission in its early years through their classes and bands (cells) where members discipled each other, prayed for each other, held each other accountable, and sent each other out into the world to witness. Perhaps a group in a corps could do something similar, maybe even work together in a common missional ministry—say, serving poor families in the neighborhood— and also bring new people into their group, including some they have actually ministered to, until the group, like a cell, divides in two with one of the groups perhaps starting a new colony of Christ in the community. These missional communities of lay Salvationists could have an agreed upon Rule of Life as suggested by Elaine Heath and Larry Duggins (*Missional. Monastic. Mainline.*). Perhaps the Rule of Life could be modeled on our Soldiers' Covenant. Members would be accountable to one another and to the corps officer. Cells would continue to split into new cells, mission would grow exponentially, and the Kingdom of God would expand significantly. Remember, the Methodist church in the West began to decline in proportion to decline of such small groups.

Reggie McNeal says we live in an increasingly non-congregational time. More and more people, he says, are not susceptible to becoming "church people who align their spiritual journeys with the goals and rhythms of organized congregational church." They're more interested in "church *lived out* in the community" (Foreword to *On the Verge*, pp. 13-14). In other words, we may be entering an era when small missional communities are more suitable to the task of both making disciples and doing mission.

If McNeal and others like him are right, and if the Army (meaning the corps) were to respond to this new reality, what would a corps then look like? It would mean that a corps would function more and more like what Hirsch calls a missional hub. It would anchor smaller missional communities or missional teams. Depending on the corps makeup and the missional targets, there might be missional teams for one, a few, or all of the following: reaching and discipling the homeless, or Sunday morning worshipers, or seniors, or young adults, or families, or children, or teens, or (fill in the blank _____). Such teams would be accountable to the corps officer(s) and the corps council. The teams would work with each other for both coordination and missional partnering. At some point in time, there could be a team working to plant a new discipling/worshiping/serving community—or to use an Army term, an *outpost*. Eventually this outpost could either become a corps itself, or it could plant another outpost.

The challenge organizationally would be to come up with ways to measure and celebrate what is happening in mission primarily outside the corps walls—how to measure a mission that takes church to the people where they are. An even deeper question is: Are we secure enough to exchange "command and control" for "support and hold accountable"? Another question is: Can we free ourselves to support both corps that are centralized and those that are de-centralized? Also, can we support a strong, centralized corps becoming a hub for decentralized mission as well—in other words, can we have both?

What is clear for the Army in the West is that what we are currently doing is leading to decline overall. What is not entirely clear is what will now begin to turn our missional ship around. My own hope is that this book will help to stimulate and resource the kind of Spirit led conversations that will guide us to the future to which our Lord is beckoning us and for which the Spirit will empower us. Christ stands at the door of your corps and mine, inviting us to the future. At no time in our history has it been more crucial for us to see Him, hear Him, and do His bidding.

FOR REFLECTION & PRAYER

Which Scripture verse or passage in the chapter spoke most deeply to you, or challenged you most? Say why.

Make, develop, and keep making disciples

Personal: Describe your own discipleship growth plan.

How well does your discipleship integrate your own personal spiritual growth, your participation in the formation of your corps' spiritual growth, and your service and witness in your life in the world during the week?

Your corps: What suggestion might you have to help your corps:

- Make discipling a never ending agenda for every person in the corps?

- Help Salvationists see every dimension and location of their lives as opportunities to live faithfully as a disciple of Jesus?

Learn how to grow organically

Personal: Is there any aspect of your life that if either trimmed or eliminated would make your life as a disciple more fruitful? If so, what would it be?

Your corps: Is there a program or a tradition in your corps that, if trimmed or changed or eliminated, could help the corps be more focused or effective as a discipleship and discipling community? If so, what is that program or tradition, and exactly what action would you recommend be taken? With whom should you discuss such action?

Learn how to grow the mission

Personal: What particular metaphor of organic growth in this section of the chapter gave you better insight into how you can personally grow your own mission effectiveness? Please describe.

Your corps: What step(s) could your corps take to move beyond the model of growth by addition to explore ways to grow by multiplication?

Be willing to colonize

Personal: Is there a group or program you are a part of in your corps that could now or in time divide to reach more people and expand discipling opportunities? If so, how would you approach suggesting that the group could become a means to reach and disciple more people? What role could you play in the colonizing?

Or, would you like to be a part of bringing together a cell for implementing a new missional initiative? What other persons in the corps could you partner with to make this reality? How would you insure accountability?

Your corps: Are there disciples in your corps who could explore together the possibility of starting an outpost in a community populated primarily by marginalized people? If so, what would the community be, and who in the corps could lead the way? What would you own role be?

WORKS CITED

Barth, Markus. *The Broken Wall: A Study of the Epistle to the Ephesians*. Philadelphia: The Judson Press, 1959.

Booth, William. *In Darkest England and the Way Out*. New York: Funk and Wagnalls, 1890.

Booth-Tucker, Emma. *Heart Messages*. New York: The Salvation Army, 1904.

Callahan, Kennon L. *Twelve Keys to an Effective Church* (second edition). San Francisco: Jossey-Bass, 2010.

Celtic Daily Prayer: Book II. London: William Collins (HarperCollins Publishers), 2015.

The Christian Mission Magazine. London, Sept. 1878.

Collier, Richard. *The General Next to God*. Glasgow: William Collins and Son and Co., 1965.

Coutts, Frederick. *The Splendor of Holiness*. London: The Salvation Army, 1983.

Coutts, Frederick, ed. *The Armoury Commentary: The Four Gospels*. London: Hodder and Stoughton, 1973.

Day, Albert Edward. *Discipline and Discovery*. The Disciplined Order of Christ, 1961.

Dean, Harry. *Power and Glory*. London: The Salvation Army, 1956.

Drummond, Henry. *The City without a Church*. London: Hodder and Stoughton, 1893.

Edge, Lynette and Morgan, Gregory. *Partnering with God: Being a Missional Salvationist*, Eugene: Wipf and Stock, 2017.

Frost, Robert. "Two Tramps in Mud Time," *The Poetry of Robert Frost*. Henry Holt and Company

Gladwell, Malcolm. *Outliers: The Story of Success*. New York: Little, Brown and Company, 2008.

Job, Reuben P. and Shawchuck, Norman, editors. *A Guide to Prayer*. Nashville: The Upper Room, 1983.

Heath, Elaine and Duggins, Larry. *Missional. Monastic. Mainline.* Eugene: Cascade Books, 2014.

Hill, Harold. *Leadership in The Salvation Army: A Case Study in Clericalisation*. Milton Keynes, U.K.: Paternoster, 2006.

Hirsch, Alan. *The Forgotten Ways: Reactivating Apostolic Movements* (second edition). Grand Rapids: Brazos Press, 2016.

Hirsch, Alan and Ferguson, Dave. *On the Verge: A Journey into the Apostolic Future of the Church*. Grand Rapids: Zondervan, 2011.

Howard, T. Henry. *Fuel for Sacred Fire*. London: The Salvation Army, 1924.

Inglis, K. S. *Churches and the Working Classes in Victorian England*. London: Routledge and Kegan Paul, 1963.

Kung, Hans. *The Church*. Translated by Ray and Rosaleen Ockenden. London: Continuum (imprint of Burns and Oates), 1967.

Law, William. *A Serious Call to a Devout and Holy Life*. London: Macmillan and Company, 1898.

MacDonald, George. *Creation in Christ: Unspoken Sermons*. Vancouver: Regent College Publishing, 1976.

Ibid. *Diary of an Old Soul*. Minneapolis: Augsburg, 1975.

Nouwen, Henri. *The Living Reminder*. New York: HarperOne, 1977.

Sandall, Robert. *The History of The Salvation Army* (volume II). London: Thomas Nelson and Sons, Ltd., 1950.

Servants Together: Salvationist Perspectives on Ministry. London: The Salvation Army, International Headquarters, 2002.

Snyder, Howard A. *The Community of the King* (revised edition). Downers Grove: IVP Academic, 2004.

The Song Book of The Salvation Army (SBSA) (2015 edition). Alexandria: USA National Headquarters.

Tennent, Timothy. "Four Wesleyan Doctrines," internet.

Tugwell, Simon. *Prayer in Practice*. Springfield: Templegate Publishers, 1974.

Waldron, John D. *The Privilege of All Believers*. Toronto: The Salvation Army, 1981.

Wall, Phil. www.infinitumlife.com.

Watson, Bernard. *Soldier Saint: George Scott Railton*. London: Hodder and Stoughton, 1970.

Winekoop, Mildred Bangs. *A Theology of Love: The Dynamic of Wesleyanism* (revised edition). Nashville: Nazarene Publishing House, 2015.